Long Ears and Short Tales

Christmas Stories

Peggy Vurgason

LONG EARS AND SHORT TALES
CHRISTMAS STORIES

iUniverse books may be ordered through booksellers or by contacting:

iUniverse
1663 Liberty Drive
Bloomington, IN 47403
www.iuniverse.com
844-349-9409

ISBN: 978-1-6632-5325-5 (sc)
ISBN: 978-1-6632-5326-2 (e)

Library of Congress Control Number: 2023911560

Print information available on the last page.

iUniverse rev. date: 07/12/2023

This is dedicated to all those who have
loved a donkey, mule, or horse.

Special thanks to my friend
Judy Salcewicz, for being my writing coach.

Contents

A Donkey's Journey 1

A New Life in Texas.. 21

Christmas Homecoming.. 43

The Barnyard Nativity... 58

Jeremiah And Starlight 70

Lizzie's Lesson 83

Papeta's Performance... 96

Sir William's Delivery 110

A Donkey's Journey

olly pulled her wool cap down over her ears as she sat in the donkey cart at the end of her driveway. Her donkey Sophie, put her ears back and listened to her.

"The kids will be excited when they get off the school bus. They have two full weeks of Christmas vacation."

Sophie quickly turned her head and stared at the opposite end of the pasture. With her big ears pointed straight up, she brayed softly.

Dolly stood up in the cart and peered in the same direction. "Bonnie and Clyde are stretching their heads over the fence." She sat down, then urged Sophie to step up so she could see down the road. "It looks like our new neighbor has made friends with our mules." She smiled as she observed the woman taking delight in petting the mules.

Dolly rubbed her chin and thought for a moment. She heard the family had suffered hardships, but she didn't know all the details. She did know, she would do whatever she could to help them. The house they lived in was owned by Sal Russo, an investor, who Dolly knew from church.

"There must be a way we can help," she told the donkey as the school bus drove up with the lights flashing.

Maddie and Micky, her five year old twin grandchildren, stepped off the bus waving back to the other children.

"This is my donkey," Micky proudly hollered.

"Sophie belongs to all of us!" Maddie corrected him.

"Whatever," Micky quickly responded then pointed to the new neighbor children staring out the school bus window. "Nonna, Jason said there's no such person as Santa Claus!"

Maddie chimed in, "Everybody knows that's not true. His sister Connie, is in my class, and she said there is a Santa but he can't come to their house this year." The child looked up at her with questioning eyes. "Nonna, could that be true?"

"She really said that?" Dolly answered and kept her eyes fixed on the school bus as it drove to the next stop.

Two children stepped off the bus and greeted their mother. The boy noticed Dolly and the children sitting in the donkey cart. Dolly waved, then the boy slowly waved back before turning his attention to his mother.

Dolly bit her bottom lip and thought for a second. "Let's jog down and introduce Sophie to the new neighbors."

"Nonna, are you going to tell Jason the truth about Santa Claus?" Micky pleaded.

"I don't think so," Dolly mumbled as she tried to think of what she would say.

"Hi Neighbor, I'm Dolly, I live in the farm across the street. Welcome to the neighborhood!"

The woman looked at the ground before looking back at her. "It's nice to meet you. My name is Loretta Smalls." She paused for a moment before speaking again. "The mules must be yours. They're beautiful."

"Yes, thank you." Dolly smiled as a thought suddenly came to her. "Would you folks like to join our church on Christmas Eve for some Christmas caroling? The mules are pulling all of us in a covered wagon." As Dolly spoke, she noticed the woman's sad eyes look away from her. She put her arms around her children and pulled them closer.

"I appreciate the offer, but my husband, Dennis, is in a wheelchair, and I can't leave him home alone." She looked in the direction of her house, then gave a quick glance back at Dolly. "It was nice meeting you." Keeping her arms around her children, she quickly walked toward her house. Dolly heard a man's angry voice calling for her.

"We're coming," Loretta answered, then turned to see if Dolly was watching.

Dolly put her head down and pretended not to have heard. She pressed her lips together as she turned the donkey cart around. "There must be something I can do," she mumbled.

For a few moments, the grandchildren sat quietly, then Micky spoke up. "Nonna, I don't think they like us very much."

Dolly took her grandson's hand in her hand. "I think they're upset right now because they moved to a new town and miss all their old friends."

Micky looked up at her with sad eyes. "Why didn't you tell Jason there really is a Santa?"

Dolly spoke in a soft sympathetic voice trying to think of an explanation the kids would believe. "Maybe Jason thinks since they moved so far away, Santa will have trouble finding them."

Both of the children, crinkled their foreheads and looked up at her. Dolly shook her head, trying to think of something that would distract them.

"Let's not talk about this because we know Santa will find them."

"Why can't we talk about it?" Micky peered up at her.

Dolly put her finger to her lips, "because it's a secret."

"Nonna, what secret?" Maddie questioned.

"I'm going to talk to Santa myself and make sure he has directions to their new house."

Both children covered their mouths with their eyes glaring. Micky whispered to Maddie, "Nonna knows Santa Claus, but don't tell anyone."

Dolly put her finger to her lips, "Remember, it's a secret."

Dolly fixed a snack for her grandchildren and placed it on a table in front of the television. "I don't want either one of you to come into my office. Nonna has some very important work to do."

"Are you calling Santa Claus now?" Micky spoke up.

Dolly put her finger to her lips again. "It's a secret, but if you leave this room, Santa will be upset with you."

"We will stay here, Nonna," Maddie answered. "Won't we Micky?"

"We'll behave, Nonna," Micky answered as he bit into a cookie.

Dolly stepped into her office and closed the door. Her first call was to Sal Russo to find out what she could about this family. Sal was also a member of the Knights of Columbus, a Catholic men's group dedicated to helping those in need. Dolly was a member of the Columbiette, the women's auxiliary to the Knights.

"Hi Dolly," Sal sounded pleased to hear from her. "I planned on giving you a call this evening."

"About our Christmas Eve caroling?" Dolly sighed, a little inpatient.

"Actually, not about that." Sal cleared his throat. "It's about my cousins. I set them up in one of my houses." Sal paused. "It's the house down the road from you."

"I met Loretta and her two children today." Dolly got right to the point. "What's their story? I can tell something's wrong."

"Yeah," Sal hesitated. "I know Dennis lost his job in New York state, then tried to start a construction company on his own. He had a bad fall, wasn't insured and they have no money. He can't walk and he needs back surgery."

"That's why I was calling you. We need to help them."

"The Knights have a plan to give them a Christmas, but first we need to get them out of the house. I was hoping you could pick them up in the covered wagon and they would join us Christmas caroling."

Dolly cut in, "I tried that already. The woman said her husband was in a wheelchair and she couldn't leave him home alone."

"Oh," Sal grumbled. "We could get him on the covered wagon. I spoke with a couple of the Knights who are willing to build a wheelchair ramp into the wagon."

Dolly paused, then continued. "As she was hurrying back to the house, I could hear her husband yelling for her. And he didn't sound too happy."

"I....know....Dennis is miserable. He's been through a lot and he can't work until he gets his back fixed. I've connections with a chief surgeon who also happens to be a Knight. He's making arrangements to get this surgery done."

"That's wonderful news!" Dolly shouted.

"Meanwhile, we only have a few days before Christmas, and I need your help getting them out of the house."

"Well, perhaps you can talk to him. He's your cousin."

"I'm going to their house tomorrow with the electrician. I'll ask him about getting on the covered wagon. If that doesn't work, then I'll tell him I need to get the house exterminated and they need to leave for awhile."

Sal and Dolly laughed, then she continued. "But what do you have planned once they're out of the house?"

"The Knights will go in with a Christmas tree, decorations, food and presents. I also have someone coming to pick up their van and take it to a repair shop. I know Loretta was looking for a job, but now their van isn't working and she would have no way of getting to work."

"The ladies will help. What can we do?"

Sal chuckled. "Actually I was going to call upon you ladies for help. The Knights will pay for all of this, but perhaps the Columbiettes can do the shopping." Sal cleared his throat. "Ladies are always better at shopping."

"This is exciting," Dolly burst into laughter. "They'll have a Christmas after all!"

Maddie and Micky looked at each other with wide eyes.

"Nonna is talking to Santa!" Maddie whispered. Both children ran to the office and put their ear to the door. When the phone call ended, they ran back to their chairs.

The next morning Loretta was serving breakfast to her family when she noticed she accidentally purchased rye bread with seeds instead of rye bread without seeds.

"Oh darn it all," she chuckled trying to keep a sense of humor as she explained her error to her family. "Maybe I need glasses when I go shopping."

"I guess you do," her husband snapped back at her. "I guess I won't have any toast this morning."

"I'll make you something else," she said in a matter of fact tone.

"Kids, today is a good day to gather pine cones and cut some branches of evergreen and holly. We can start decorating for Christmas with what we have here in the yard."

"Will Santa Clause come if we decorate?" Connie pleaded.

Loretta's eyes grew misty. "I don't know, Sweetheart."

"I don't believe in Santa," Jason cut in.

"Don't say that," Loretta snapped at her son.

"When we are finished eating we will ALL go outside," Loretta announced and glanced at her husband. "Kids, you and I will be in the back of the house finding things to decorate with. Dennis, since I can't push you very far outside, you can sit in the front of the house and feed the birds that loaf of rye bread with seeds.

Dennis sat alone in the front yard knowing his poor behavior upset his wife. He broke the bread into little pieces and threw it on the ground. Surely the birds wouldn't come near him to eat. "They will come when I go back into the house," he thought. "I'll watch them from the window." He stopped breaking the bread for a few moments and stared at the birds. "I won't hurt you. You can come close to me and pick up these crumbs."

Then for the fist time in several months, he put his head down and prayed. "Lord, I'm not taking these hardships too well, am I?" He rubbed his forehead recalling his irate behavior that morning and every morning, every afternoon, and every evening. "Lord help me please. I don't want to be like this. Please show me a sign You are listening."

Just as he finished his prayer, he heard footsteps approaching.

He knew his family was in the backyard, and quickly opened his eyes.

"What in the world?" He mumbled as a donkey approached him. The donkey brayed softly with her long ears pointing directly at him.

Suddenly his heart felt lighter and a smile formed across his face. "Where did you come from?"

The donkey put her nose in his lap and sniffed the bread. "Would you like some of this bread?"

Before he could get the words out, the donkey took a slice and ate it.

"Well, you're not shy!" Dennis chuckled and handed the donkey another piece of bread. He watched with amusement as the donkey shook her head up and down as she ate. When she was finished chewing, she looked straight at Dennis and raised her upper lip. Dennis didn't know she was reacting to the seeds in the bread and thought the donkey was laughing at him.

The donkey took more bread, ate it, then raised her lip again. For the first time in a long time, Dennis burst into laughter. He continued giving the donkey bread, and the donkey continued to eat it and raise her upper lip. Dennis laughed so hard, tears ran down his cheeks.

Loretta and the children stopped what they were doing and listened. Loretta's eyes lit up and she put her hand across her mouth.

"Is something wrong with Daddy?" Connie asked.

"Is he laughing or crying?" Jason questioned, "Because I never hear him laugh like that anymore."

Loretta's face reddened. She wanted to see her husband

laughing again, but she was afraid of what she might find if he wasn't truly laughing.

Jason ran to the front of the house and was the first to see his father with the donkey. The donkey continued eating the bread from Dennis's hand and raising her lip. Dennis was laughing so hard, he was stopping his feet and his face was wet with tears.

Jason turned to his mother and sister. Loretta's hands were folded at her chest, while his sister just looked on with astonishment. "Isn't this Maddie and Micky's donkey?"

"I think so," Connie responded, "but why is she here?"

Loretta swallowed, then put her hand on Connie's shoulder. "She probably broke out of the pasture. We should go tell Miss Dolly she's here."

"I'll go," Jason turned and started walking.

"I don't think you should walk by yourself. I'll go with you." Loretta lowered her head to Connie, "You stay here with Daddy. Jason and I will be right back."

Dolly was finishing her morning barn chores when she noticed the mules looking over the fence from the corner of the pasture. She didn't see Sophie, but she assumed she was standing in front of the big mules and out of her view.

"Maybe the neighbors are feeding them treats again," she thought. "Anything to make them smile." She shook her head and called her yellow lab. "Come on Charlie, let's go get the mail and see what the mules are looking at." Dolly and Charlie hopped in the pickup truck. After getting the mail, Dolly drove to the end of the pasture where the mules were standing. She noticed the fence was broken at the bottom and Sophie wasn't standing where she expected.

"Oh great," she mumbled, then recognized Loretta and Jason waving their hands and walking toward her.

"Your donkey is at our house!" Jason yelled to her.

Dolly drove her truck to meet up with them. "I am sorry, I hope she isn't bothering you. She's never gotten out before." As she was speaking, she noticed the excitement in their faces.

"She's fine," Loretta smiled at her and put her hand on Dolly's arm. "She made friends with my husband."

There was something in the woman's eyes, that told Dolly making friends with her husband was very special.

"I'll come back with the cart and harness so I can drive her home. My husband, Pete can drive the truck back. Give me a few minutes to load everything on this pickup truck."

Loretta squeezed Dolly's arm and giggled. "There's no hurry. Really."

Dolly giggled back at her. "All right, I'll take my time." Loretta's eyes filled with tears and she gave Dolly's arm another squeeze.

"It looks like Sophie made a new friend," Pete commented as he observed Dennis's radiant smile while scratching Sophie's head and neck. Sophie stood very close to the wheelchair with her eyes closed, enjoying the moment.

"Hi!" Dennis looked up at Pete and Dolly, and chuckled. "Your little donkey likes me!"

"I see that," Pete smiled warmly at Dennis then extended his hand. "My name is Pete and this is my wife Dolly."

"I'm Dennis," he returned the warm smile, then introduced his family.

"Would you like a ride in the donkey cart?" Dolly offered.

"I don't know," Dennis chuckled. "Can she pull us both?"

"Of course," Dolly answered, then turned to the children. "Would you like a ride too?"

Both children jumped up and down clapping their hands.

Pete helped Dennis maneuver from the wheelchair to the cart. As he settled into the seat, he smiled brightly at his wife and children.

"Step up," Dolly tapped the reins and the cart jolted forward.

"Oh!" Dennis laughed and gripped the side of the cart. As Sophie trotted off, Dennis looked back at his wife and children. They were laughing with him and waving 'good-bye'.

"Daddy's having fun," Connie pressed her hands together and looked up at her mother.

"You must come to our farm and meet Bonnie and Clyde," Dolly spoke in a matter of fact tone to Dennis.

"Bonnie and Clyde?" Dennis's face lit up. "Some type of gangsters?"

"Not really gangsters," Dolly laughed. "They are huge mules, who used to pull hay wagons."

"I'd love to meet them!" He laughed keeping a grip on the side of the cart.

"Great!" Dolly turned abruptly and faced him. She told him the plans to go Christmas caroling on the covered wagon. "We'll pick you guys up around 4:00!"

"I'd love that!" His eyes beamed.

After she finished giving Dennis a ride, she gave the children a ride, then Loretta a ride.

As Loretta was getting out of the cart, Sal pulled into the driveway with the electrician.

"Dolly and Pete!," Sal chuckled. "What brings you guys here?"

"Sophie decided to sneak out and meet the Smalls family." Dolly announced.

"Okay…" Sal answered with a questioning look.

Dolly moved closer to him and whispered. "They're coming caroling with us!"

Sal grabbed a hold of her hand. "Good job! I'll call you later."

Dolly drove Sophie back to the farm and Pete followed in the truck. The donkey jogged with her head held high, aware of the good fate she brought to the ailing neighbor.

When they arrived back at their barn, Pete got out of the truck and walked toward the equipment shed and shouted over his shoulder to Dolly. "Don't unhitch her yet. I'll get a few tools then we'll drive along the fence and find the spot where she escaped."

"Sounds good," Dolly responded, then scratched Sophie on her rump.

Sophie turned her head toward Dolly and chattered her teeth as she enjoyed being scratched.

As Pete hammered the fence post, Bonnie and Clyde stood a few feet away and watched every move he made. When Pete finished, the mules followed him back to the barn, then focused on the sound of another hammer.

"Who's there?" Dolly spoke in a puzzled tone, then noticed a pickup truck and two men doing something with wood near the covered wagon.

"Hi Dolly and Pete," a familiar voice answered. Then Mason, one of the Knights, came out of the shed. "Sorry if I frightened you. Tom and I are building a handicap ramp for Sal's cousin."

Dolly laughed with excitement, while Pete commented "Sal didn't waste any time. Did he?"

"No Sir, he didn't. We'll be out of here in a couple of hours."

"It's okay," Pete assured him. "Come up to the house for coffee when you're finished."

"When Dolly got back to the house, the phone was ringing and she raced across the room to answer it.

"Dolly, how did you convince my cousin to go Christmas caroling on the covered wagon?" He shouted with excitement.

"I did't do anything to convince him. I only invited him and he gladly accepted. I think it was the donkey who gave him a change of heart."

Then Dolly explained how the donkey journeyed to entertain Dennis.

"How about that!" Sal was intrigued.

"Donkeys are smart!" Dolly made her point. "Sophie knew someone needed a laugh and she knew what to do to make it happen!"

"That's unbelievable!" Sal shouted again. "I would have never guessed that any animal would be that smart."

Dolly raised her eyebrows. "The donkey is the most mentioned animal in the Bible. Balaam's donkey saw the angel in the road, then spoke to Balaam."

"All right I believe you," Sal chuckled, then spoke in a serious tone. "The Knights purchased a turkey with fixings for Christmas dinner and other groceries for them to stock up. We have a tree and decorations, "Sal paused. "We will give you money to shop for presents."

Dolly giggled. "When I was giving them a ride in the cart, I sized each one up to determine their clothes size. I'll go out tonight and get started."

"You are on the ball!" Sal praised her. "Bring everything to my house and I will reimburse you. A couple of the ladies will go to the house with us, and help decorate and do whatever else needs to be done."

"Sounds like a plan," Dolly concluded.

The afternoon of Christmas Eve, Dolly and Pete hitched up their two mules and headed down the road for their neighbor's house. A caravan of Knights and Columbiettes, stayed behind waiting for the right time to make their move.

"Nonna, do you really think Santa will miss Connie and Jason's house tonight?" Maddie pleaded from the first seat.

"I'm sure Santa will stop at their house tonight," Dolly turned her head and smiled at her granddaughter.

"You called Santa on the telephone, didn't you Nonna?" Micky cut in.

Dolly and Pete looked at each other and chuckled.

Pete spoke up. "Nonna and I know Santa personally, but we won't talk about this tonight. Okay?"

"Why not?" Both children pleaded.

"Let them be surprised tomorrow when they open all their presents." Pete gave a little wink.

The twins looked at each other with wide eyes. "Won't they be surprised?" Micky chuckled. "Because Jason said there's no such thing as Santa Clause."

As they drove the wagon into the neighbor's yard, Jason waved from the porch then opened the front door and announced, "They're here! Let's go everybody!"

As Loretta pushed the wheelchair across the lawn, Pete set up the new handicap ramp on the wagon.

"Wow!" Dennis exclaimed. "Look at this craftsmanship," he

pointed to the ramp on the wagon. He asked Loretta to move him closer for a better look.

"Compliments of a couple of our Brother Knights," Pete proudly stated, then showed him how the ramp is stored under the wagon when not in use.

Dennis beamed with pride. "Some careful planning was put into that."

Minutes later the wagon was headed for town, where they would meet up with a group of carolers in the church parking lot. The planned course, was to carol down main street, then stop at the assistant living and nursing home. The wagon would then bring the carolers back to the church parking lot, then drive home.

Pete sent a text message to Sal telling him the house was out of view and it was time to move in.

"Lets' roll!" Sal gave the command. The engines sounded and the operation began. A pickup truck with a Christmas tree and two bicycles led the way. Next in line was a van loaded with food and presents, followed by a tow truck.

The first order of business was to hook up Loretta's van to the tow truck that would take it to the repair shop. When that was done, the men carried the tree and the bicycles into the house. Sal hung Christmas lights along the porch, around the windows and around a big tree in the yard.

Jane and Patty were busy putting the food away, arranging the presents, hanging the stockings and decorating the tree.

Jack, another Knight, set up a life-size plastic Nativity scene on the lawn. Inside the stable, Baby Jesus laid in a manger with Mary and Joseph kneeling at His sides. A gray donkey stood guard outside, looking in at the Baby Jesus.

A couple of hours later, Sal stood in the kitchen rubbing his hands together. "We have everything done outside, how are you ladies making out in here?"

"I believe we are finished in here as well," Jane turned to him holding an angel ornament. "I just need someone tall enough to place her on the tree top."

"I'll do the honors," Jack came in the doorway.

Sal looked up at Jack who stood 6'5". "I think you are the right man for the job," Sal chuckled.

"Any word from Chris about the van?" Jack asked.

Sal looked at his watch, "It's still early. Chris said it would take about two to three hours to do everything. There's still time. Chris will send a text when the van is on the way back here."

Jane took a deep breath. "This is exciting, I would love to see the expression on their faces when they see everything."

Jack snapped his fingers. "We have everything except a hidden camera." Everyone looked at each other and laughed.

"If we are finished here, then Patty and I will head out," Jane said.

"What should we do now?" Jack tapped his hand on the countertop staring at the cookies.

"Just wait here," Sal sighed.

"I have a wonderful idea," Jack's eyes widened with mischief. "Maybe we should sample some of those Christmas cookies!"

Patty turned around as she was walking out the door. "Only one cookie each!" She chuckled, then walked with Jane to her van.

Meanwhile, the carolers and the assisted living residents were having a wonderful time.

"I'm sorry if we seem a bit unorganized." Mrs. Fenton, the

receptionist took a hold of Loretta's hand. "We're short help right now."

"This is so much fun," Loretta beamed as she observed Jason pushing his father in the wheelchair.

"Do you know anyone who would be interested in a job here?" Mrs. Fenton whispered in her ear.

Loretta's face lit up, "I need a job." Then her face fell as she remembered her van was out of order. "I'll need transportation until I earn enough money to get my van fixed."

Mrs. Fenton patted Loretta's hand, "Let me know when you can start." Then she walked back to her desk.

Loretta closed her eyes and whispered, "Thank You Jesus."

It was dark when the carolers got out of the wagon at the church parking lot. A Mercedes-Benz pulled up close to it. The window rolled down; a middle aged man poked his head out and looked around the wagon. "I'm looking for Dennis Smalls."

Dennis and Loretta looked at each other with their mouths open.

Singling the man out in the wheelchair, he said, "Are you Dennis?"

"Yes Sir," Dennis looked around, then blinked. "I'm Dennis."

"Dennis, I'm Dr. Wells, one of the Knights." He paused and cleared his throat. "Can I come on board and talk to you?" Then he looked at Dolly and Pete and nodded.

Dolly nudged Pete. "That's means, 'talk privately'."

"Oh," Pete quickly stood up as Dolly beckoned to her grandchildren.

Loretta grabbed Dennis's hand as the doctor climbed into the wagon.

Dr. Wells put one hand on Dennis's shoulder and shook

Dennis's hand with his other hand. Then he shook Loretta's hand and sat down. "I understand you had an accident and need surgery."

Dennis and Loretta looked at each other. Loretta's face flushed as she spoke, "Dr. Wells, we are not able to pay…"

The doctor put his hand up. "It's all taken care of."

Loretta covered her mouth and gasped. Dennis put his head down not knowing what to say.

"It's what we Knights do." The doctor stood up and handed his card to Loretta. "Call me the day after Christmas and we'll get you in as soon as possible so you can have your life back."

Loretta put her head down and sobbed. The doctor patted her on the shoulder. "Merry Christmas and God Bless you both." He climbed down from the wagon and waved to Pete and Dolly.

"Merry Christmas," Pete and Dolly waved back.

As the wagon was leaving town, a tow truck passed them.

"There goes our van!" Jason shouted.

"That's not your van," Pete shouted back, then winked at Dolly.

"Yes it was!" Jason argued. "I know our blue van. It has Mom's blue rosary beads hanging from the mirror."

Pete chuckled. "That wasn't rosary beads in the mirror. It was .. a… name tag."

Dolly started giggling as Jason continued to argue. "Mom didn't you see our van?"

Loretta started to answer, when Dolly turned around and put her finger to her lips. As Dolly tried to hold back the laughter, tears rolled down her cheeks.

"I'm afraid to guess about the van," Loretta giggled and put both arms around her husband's arm.

As the wagon turned onto their road, an empty tow truck was heading in the opposite direction.

"That's the same tow truck," Jason yelled. "I bet they brought our van back!" Then he yelled to Pete, "Can't these mules go any faster?"

"Not really," Pete turned to him. "But we are almost home."

After the wagon turned around the bend, Christmas lights and the Nativity scene came into view.

"That's our house!" Jason jumped up from his seat.

"It is our house!" Connie joined him. "I see a big Christmas tree through the window!"

"And presents, lots of presents!" Jason shouted.

Tears sprang to Loretta's eyes, and she put her head on Dennis's shoulder.

"Mommy, Daddy," Connie cried. "Santa did come after all! I knew he would! I just knew it!"

"I told you Santa was for real," Micky chimed in, while Maddie took Connie's hand and giggled.

"How can I thank you enough for all you have done?" Loretta sobbed as Dolly gave her a hug.

"Our van is back," Jason shouted again. "There's a big red bow and a note on it."

As Jason ran to the van, Pete set the wheelchair ramp in place, then pushed Dennis to read the note.

The note read: "Van is fixed with new parts and new tires, Merry Christmas, The Knights of Columbus."

Dennis looked up at Pete with tears in his eyes. "My cousin had something to do with this I'm sure."

"It's what we Knights and Columbiettes do," Pete whispered

modestly, then turned the wheelchair toward the Nativity scene where Loretta and the children were staring.

Connie put her hand on the donkey, "This looks like Sophie!"

"Sophie, the visiting donkey." Loretta smiled. "These past few days have been a real transformation with everything that has happened," Loretta struggled with the words, as she held back the tears. "Everything was awful, just awful. Then it all changed with a donkey's journey to our house."

"Merry Christmas," Dolly waved to the family, then beckoned to her grandchildren to get back in the wagon. She began turning the team around while Pete walked the family to their door.

As the mules were making the turn, they stopped to sniff the plastic donkey. Dolly laughed and let them sniff.

Pete got back in the wagon and looked at his grandchildren, "Did you have a good time?"

"Yes," they both answered. Then Maddie questioned, "Nonno, why did Santa come to their house before they went to bed?"

Dolly and Pete looked at each other, then Micky answered. "Santa had to use a GPS because they moved."

"Sounds about right," Dolly chuckled. "Since they moved, everything has been different for them." She took a deep breath and continued. "Everything was made new after a donkey's journey to their house."

She smiled back at her grandchildren, "Merry Christmas."

A New Life in Texas

"I think we are on the final stretch," Sal huffed as he drove along the county road in Plantersville Texas.

His wife, Maria, quickly opened her eyes and sat up straight. "It's been so long since I've been here." She opened the window and took a deep breath. "Oh the smell of cedar trees." She smiled, then reached back and tapped her daughter. "Patty, wake up."

Her poodle, Snickers, jumped down from her lap, wagging his tail."

"Are we there yet?" Patty rubbed her eyes and yawned.

"A few more minutes," Maria rubbed Snickers' head.

It was a couple of weeks before Christmas. They had driven from NJ in an older Winnebago, with their family car in tow. Trying to put the long hard year behind them, they were ready to begin a new life on a ranch in Texas. It was a ranch that Maria recently inherited from her grandfather.

"This is it!" Maria moved closer to window.

Sal hesitated, then turned into the driveway of their new home. A lump formed in his throat.

Patty peered out the window. She was fourteen years old and

happy with her life in New Jersey. She was not happy about the move to Texas.

Sal owned a restaurant in NJ for twenty five years. Sal Defano's Italian Food was well known for a good Italian meal. The family lived a comfortable life in a plush apartment above the restaurant. As everything changes in time, the neighborhood became infested with drugs and crime. Their business went downhill, and so did their bank account.

The family had no other choice but to sell everything and move. The city purchased the restaurant building and turned it into offices. After paying all of their debts, there was little money left for them to start over. They didn't want to move away from family and friends, but it seemed the timing of the inheritance was God Sent.

Over the next few days the family continued to unpack and organize their new home. Patty found the barn very interesting. It was something very new to her. Animals had not lived there for several years, but the barn tools and equipment still remained.

"When can we get farm animals?" Patty anxiously asked as Snickers walked around the barn sniffing.

"Animals cost money." Maria sighed, then smiled at her daughter, "After we find jobs, we will buy animals."

Patty rolled her eyes then plopped down on a dusty bale of hay.

"We will make this work," Maria tried to sound cheerful and glanced around the barn with wide eyes. Suddenly a huge smile formed across her face. "Oh," she blurted out, then hurried toward an object covered with cobwebs.

"This was Pixie's cart!" Maria grabbed a broom and gently began to remove the cobwebs.

"Who was Pixie?" Patty asked as she shielded her face from the dust.

"Pixie was a special donkey. She used to pull this little red cart in horse shows." Maria stepped back from the cart and brushed the dust from her clothes. "Someplace there's a trunk filled with her trophies and ribbons."

"Okay…" Patty walked to the barn door and peered out. "There are donkeys on the farm across the street." Standing up on her toes, she continued, "The sign says 'Jerry's Rescue Donkey Ranch'." She looked back at her mother "What is a rescue ranch?"

"A rescue ranch is a place for animals that need homes. Jerry must be a good person if all of those donkeys are rescued. One day soon, we should go across the street and introduce ourselves."

After dinner, Patty said "Good night," to her parents and walked down the hall to her new bedroom. She didn't feel like sleeping, but she did want to be alone.

"If only I had a reason to go across the street and meet Jerry," she thought. "I'd ask him for a job."

Patty rolled over on her back and stared at the ceiling trying to come up with a plan. Snickers jumped up on her shoulder and started licking her chin.

"Put your thinking cap on, Snickers. There must be some reason for us to go over there."

Just then a soft wind rocked the tree branches against her bedroom window. Snickers started barking and jumped off the bed and ran to the window.

"It's just the wind," Patty closed her eyes as she spoke. Her little dog paid no attention to her and tried to jump up on the windowsill.

"That's it!" Patty opened her eyes and jumped off the bed. She scooped Snickers up in her arms and pressed him to her chest. "You just gave me an idea!"

It was Saturday morning and Christmas was only a few days away. After breakfast, Patty put her jacket on and walked toward the door with Snickers under her arm. "I'm going for a walk. I won't be too long."

"Any place in particular?" her father inquired.

"Not really," she answered without looking at him. "I just want to take a walk and look around."

"Be careful. The cars move pretty fast on these roads," he warned.

"Don't let Snickers wander," her mother added.

Patty walked to the end of the driveway and turned right toward the sign that read, "Jerry's Rescue Ranch."

As she approached, she saw a man throwing hay over the fence to the donkeys. A dog stood a few feet away from the man. Snickers started barking at the other dog and squirmed out from Patty's arm. Before Patty could react, the dog bolted under the fence and onto the ranch property.

A devilish grin formed across her face as she whispered, "Good boy, Snickers." Then she opened the gate and entered the property and ran after him. The other dog noticed the intruders and started running toward the little poodle.

"Blue, Come here!" The man called to his dog who was about five times the size of Snickers.

Snickers realized that he was outmatched, and ran back to Patty. She scooped him up and stood still for a moment, not knowing what to do next.

The man was tall and thin. He had a thick black mustache and wore a black cowboy hat that shaded his face. His work jacket was unzipped, exposing a big silver belt buckle. He pet his dog's head in an effort to keep the dog still and waited for Patty to say something.

Patty took a deep breath and tried to compose herself. She came this far so she might as well speak up. "I am sorry to bother you, Mr. Jerry.... I ugh.."

The man continued staring at her, then broke into a grin. "I'm not Mr. Jerry. Jerry is still asleep. He works very late at night." He nodded his head toward the house.

As he was speaking, Snickers started barking and tried to squirm out of her arms again. Blue whined and looked up at the man. The man said something to the dog and the dog settled down.

"I wouldn't let that little dog run around here if I were you." He said in a grave tone. "Donkeys don't like strange dogs." The man and his dog continued staring at Patty and Snickers.

"I'm sorry to bother you," Patty spoke on the verge of tears. She quickly turned and ran toward the gate, holding Snickers as tightly as she could.

The man chuckled as he scratched his dog's head. "I guess we scared her. Let's get back to work."

Sal and Maria were sitting at the kitchen table when Patty burst through the door and let go of Snickers. "Oh!" She gasped without taking her hand off the doorknob.

"What happened?" Maria spoke up.

Sal quickly got up from his chair and put his arm around his daughter.

"Snickers got away from me and ran through the fence at the donkey farm. I had to run after him. There was a mean cowboy and a big dog who wanted to attack Snickers. The cowboy told me the donkeys might hurt Snickers. So I got scared and ran home."

"Did you tell him you were new in the neighborhood?" Maria asked as she brushed the hair away from her daughter's forehead.

"I was going to, but I didn't get a chance. He said Jerry was in the house sleeping." Patty wiped the tears from her eyes.

Sal pulled out a chair and motioned for her to sit. "You didn't do any harm. You are't hurt and Snickers is't hurt. Relax."

Maria sat down next to her daughter and took a hold of her hand. Purposely changing the subject, Maria pressed her lips together and raised her eyebrows. "I think it's a good day to explore the attic."

Sal started teasing, "There might be bats up there. We better have some hot chocolate first."

"What does hot chocolate have to do with bats?" Patty asked with wide eyes.

"It doesn't." Sal laughed. "I just want some hot chocolate."

"Snickers will protect us from the bats," Maria laughed then poured milk into a pot.

When they finished their hot chocolate, Maria led the way up the attic stairs. Patty walked behind her father, with Snickers in one hand and gripped the banister with the other hand. Maria opened the attic door, and turned on the lights. Her eyes widened as she gazed around the room full of cobwebs.

"Well so far I don't see any bats," she courageously turned to her daughter and husband.

"That's because they don't come out until dusk." Sal teased. "We will probably see them hanging upside down some place up here." Patty swallowed hard, then let Snickers down to explore. She stood motionless and stared at the cobwebs.

Maria slowly walked around the attic that was mostly filled with trunks. In the corner, she saw life size plastic figures covered with cobwebs and dust.

"Our Nativity Scene!" Maria folded her hands at her chest. "This meant so much to Nonno and Nonna.."

She brushed the dust away from the Blessed Mother's face, then touched each plastic character and recited its name.

When Maria came to the donkey, Sal nudged Patty and chuckled, "Well there's your donkey."

Patty rolled her eyes. "Nice try Dad."

Without any further attic exploring, the family carried the plastic figures down the attic steps.

"I have the perfect place for this," Sal pointed out the window of the family room to a dilapidated structure in the backyard. "That was probably a tool shed," Sal scratched his head. "I can turn it into a stable for the Nativity Scene."

Maria and Patty stared back at him with their mouths open. "Well come on," he said as he picked up the figure of St. Joseph. "Let's carry the set outside and see how it will fit!"

"Let's go Pat," Maria beckoned, as she lifted the figure of the Blessed Mother.

Patty let out a deep sigh and picked up the manger. Snickers sat at attention, wagging his little tail across the wooden floor. "Come on, Snickers," she commanded.

Sal spent the rest of the afternoon restructuring the tool shed into a lovely little Nativity Stable. Maria and Patty brought a bale of hay from the barn. They spread the hay on the floor and filled the manger for Baby Jesus.

Sal wiped the sweat from his brow, then gazed at the beautiful sunset. "We finished just in time. Let's turn on the lights."

Patty ran to the house and plugged the extension cord to an outlet on the porch. Maria ran after her, giggling and trying to catch her breath. "There's a switch inside." While keeping her eyes on the Nativity Scene, she flipped the switch.

Miraculously the Nativity Scene lit up and almost came to life. Patty and Maria hugged each other, then ran across the lawn to hug Sal. The three of them stood in awe gazing at the beautiful arrangement they created.

"Our first Christmas in Texas will be a good one." Maria exclaimed. "The birth of Jesus brings new life and new beginning."

Sal nodded his head and smiled at her. "Father Roco used to say that every Christmas."

"I miss Father Roco," Patty whispered.

"I miss him too," Sal put his arm around his daughter and gave her a squeeze. "I'm getting hungry. Let's have pizza delivered!"

"Sounds like a plan," Maria agreed. "We can have dinner and enjoy our Christmas creativity."

The next day Maria and Patty explored the attic for a second time. This time they found the trunk with all Maria's ribbons and trophies. They also found another trunk with Christmas tree ornaments and other Christmas items.

As Maria's eyes began to fill with tears, Patty picked up one of the trunks and headed for the stairs. "Come on Mom, Dad wants to find a tree today."

Patty wiped both trunks with a wet paper towel, then opened the Christmas trunk. On top was something wrapped in a white cloth embroidered with Christmas holly. She put it on her lap and gently unwrapped it. It was a circle made from a wire coat hanger. Four bottle caps were attached to it, spaced evenly apart. She held it up for her mother to see. "Mom?"

Maria's jaw dropped. She took the object from Patty and held it with both hands. "This is an advent wreath and doily cloth that Nonna made." Maria chuckled as she touched the bottle caps. "These are bleach bottle caps to put the candles in." She spread the white doily cloth on the round dinning room table and put the wire wreath in the center of it. "We need candles and evergreens to cover the wire." Maria sighed as she straightened the doily. "We'll get four tapers for the bottle caps and one thick white candle for the middle to light on Christmas Day."

"Why don't we just cover it with palm branches," Patty snickered.

Maria pretended not to hear her and continued unpacking the trunk.

The afternoon of Christmas Eve, Patty looked out the front window and began to feel homesick. "I can't believe this will be the first year that we won't be going to Aunt Gracie's house for Christmas lunch. It doesn't even look like Christmas here with all of the palm trees and green leaves still on the trees." She put her hand on her forehead and plopped down on the couch.

Maria and Sal stopped what they were doing in the kitchen and sat on the couch beside her.

"I know this is hard," Maria said putting her hand on the back of Patty's neck. "Things happen that we don't expect. We have each other and we have a place to live."

"Can't we sell this farm and move back to NJ?" Patty's voice was growing angry.

Maria was lost for words. Sal quickly spoke firmly to his daughter. "Maybe someday, but for now, this will be our home." Not knowing what else to say or do, he continued, "Let's go out for dinner, then we will stop at the store and get candles for the advent wreath."

Sal was trying very hard to keep the spirits up. As he drove out the driveway, he began singing Christmas carols. Maria joined in, then beckoned to her daughter. Patty brushed the hair away from her face and joined in song.

Later that night they attended Midnight Mass at their new church in town. An Irish priest, whom they had't met, sang High Mass. His tenor voice was stunning and the choir sounded like Heavenly angels.

In his sermon, Father spoke of growing up on a farm in Ireland. "My father used to tell us that the animals always knelt down very early Christmas morning. I was never in the barn that early on Christmas, but I believed him."

Maria looked over at her daughter and saw her smile as she listened to the priest. Then she noticed Sal also watching her. He looked back at Maria, then took a hold of her hand and squeezed it.

When mass was finished, the Irish priest stood at the back of the church and wished everyone a Merry Christmas. When Sal, Maria and Patty approached, he extended his hand and said, "Welcome newcomers!" They introduced themselves, and exchanged pleasures.

"I really enjoyed that," Patty smiled as they walked out to their car. "Is it true that animals really do know about Christmas?" She giggled, "It never seemed to phase Snickers; he's only interested in his Christmas stocking."

"I think Father was referring to farm animals," Maria turned and faced Patty.

Patty leaned in between her parents from the back seat. "Well maybe we could get a glimpse of Jerry's donkeys kneeling down in the pasture when we go by."

"I'll drive by slowly so you can have a look," Sal said, glancing at his daughter.

As they continued driving, Sal slowed up at each farm hoping to see the animals in the field under the cool winter starry night. To their disappointment, they were only able to see a few cows lying down in a pasture. None of Jerry's donkeys could be seen from the road.

Patty flopped back in her seat. "Oh well, so much for seeing kneeling animals."

As they pulled into their own driveway, the Nativity scene was in full view. Maria started singing 'Silent Night', then Patty and Sal joined in. As they reached the end of the driveway, it appeared that the angel on the left side of the stable began to rock back and forth.

Maria gasped, "Sal, what's going on in there?"

The shepherd boy next to the angel rocked back and forth, then the next angel tipped over and landed on top of St. Joseph.

"I think there is a rodent in the Nativity Scene," Sal drove up to the stable. Before he could get out of the car, a set of eyes filled with anguish appeared above the manger. Above the anguished eyes were two large brown ears.

"Is that a real donkey?" Patty jumped up in her seat.

"It is a real miniature donkey," Maria confirmed. "Stay in the car, I'll check it out."

Maria slowly walked toward the little donkey. As she got closer, she bent down and gently extended her hand. The donkey was panting and appeared to be in pain. She extended her nose toward Maria then laid down. Maria noticed the donkey's sides contracting and a little hoof appeared under her tail.

Tears filled Maria's eyes as she knelt down beside the little jenny and gently stroked her forehead.

"Mom what's happening?" Patty was out of the car and edging her way to the stable.

Maria beckoned, then put her finger to her lips. "Shush, she's having a baby."

Sal followed Patty into the stable.

Maria remained on her knees and continued stroking the animal and speaking gently to her. Patty put her arm around her father's arm, "She's having a baby! What should we do?"

Maria looked up at them, "Get me some towels and a blanket from the washroom, the iodine from the medicine kit, and a pail of warm water."

Patty couldn't move fast enough, but Sal just stood and stared at his wife.

"Please go help her and get back here right away so you both can witness this birth."

A minute later, Patty ran across the lawn with towels, iodine, and a blanket. Sal walked as quickly as he could, taking big steps carrying a pail of warm water.

"The nose and two feet are poking their way through," Maria whispered looking up at her husband and daughter. "Don't get too close."

Sal put the pale down inside the manger. Patty clenched the towels and blanket to her chest and whispered to her father, "This is so exciting!"

"You're doing good Mamma; just push a little more and I'll be able to help you." Maria moved closer to the donkey's tail while Sal and Patty stretched their necks to see what was going on.

The foal's head and both front feet were completely out. The donkey looked up at Maria with her big brown eyes, begging for help. Maria took a hold of the tiny feet and gently pulled the baby out of the mother and into the world.

"It's a girl!" Maria announced. "Bring a towel and help dry her."

Patty knelt down beside her mother and gently rubbed the foal with the towels. Mamma picked her head up and saw that her baby was being taken care of. She closed her eyes, and rested her head in the hay.

Maria cleaned under her tail with warm water then dried her. She put iodine on the foal where the umbilical cord was attached. Within an hour, Mamma and foal were on their feet. The foal began to nurse.

"Shouldn't we give Mamma something to eat and drink?" Patty questioned.

"I think she'd like that. Bring out the bag of carrots and box of granola cereal," Maria instructed. "There's another bucket in the wash room, fill it with water."

"My granola cereal?" Sal cut in.

"There's more at the store," Maria quickly responded without looking at him.

Maria and Patty made a bed behind the manger with the blanket and a couple of dry towels. It was the warmest part of the stable. Sal handed Maria the cereal and carrots. Mamma immediately stretched her neck and wiggled her nose toward the food. After she had enough to eat, she laid down on the bed and snuggled with her baby.

Sal wrapped an arm around each of his girls. "What a time and place to give birth," he whispered.

Maria's eyes began to sting as she stared at Mamma and baby so peacefully nestled close to the cradle of Our Lord. In spite of being so homesick, she felt the true Christmas spirit in her heart and broke into song, "*Silent Night, Holy Night....*"

Sal and Patty joined in. Their faces were wet with tears but they sang every note clearly. When they finished singing, they hugged each other.

"This is a very special Christmas miracle," Patty sobbed.

"We should go in the house now," Maria beckoned. "In the morning we can tell Jerry that one of his donkeys is here."

"You mean two of his donkeys," Patty added in comic relief.

They walked back to the house arm in arm with Sal in the middle. Lowering his head to be closer to his girls, he whispered, "I never expected anything like this to happen."

Patty and Maria, smiled and let out a sigh. The family reached the back porch, then turned their heads in silence for another look at the stable.

"A very special Christmas miracle," Sal repeated.

They went inside where Snickers was anxiously waiting for

them. Patty picked him up and scratched under his chin. "You knew something was going on outside. You're a smart little dog."

Sal turned on the Christmas tree lights and sang, "Oh Christmas tree, Oh Christmas tree." Then he turned toward the kitchen and continued singing the same melody, "Let's have some eggnog and some Christmas cookies!"

Very early the next morning, Patty jumped out of bed, quickly dressed, then tip-toed down the hall with Snickers under her arm. She thought she was the first one up, but the smell of fresh coffee told her she wasn't. "Good morning," she said cheerfully, but there was no answer. She noticed some milk spilled on the counter top near the electric coffee pot. The cutting board was in the sink with apple and carrot cuttings. There was an empty cereal box on the counter. Through the bay window, she could see both of her parents gingerly walking to the stable carrying their hot coffees, a plastic container and a pail of water.

"They're taking food out to the baby without us," she mumbled to Snickers and quickly put on her jacket and hurried after them.

Sal turned when he heard the back door open, "Merry Christmas," he chuckled raising his coffee mug. "Merry Christmas on the ranch in Texas!"

Patty ran to her father and mother and gave them both a big hug. "Merry Christmas! How's our little Christmas miracle doing this morning?"

When Mamma heard their voices, she walked out of the stable with her nose extended toward them and baby followed.

"Look at the milk around her whiskers?" Patty giggled, then grabbed a hold of her father's arm. Maria bent down and slowly extended her hand toward Mamma. Mamma walked close to Maria and sniffed her hand. Baby followed and did the same.

"She really trusts people," Maria smiled and stroked Mamma's head.

"Where should I put this food?" Sal held out the plastic container.

Immediately Mamma grabbed it with her teeth; lowered it to the ground and began munching. The baby looked at them, then continued nursing.

"She's hungry!" Sal laughed.

Patty's face lit up. "This is the best Christmas ever!"

Maria's eyes filled with tears as she put her arms around her daughter. "New life in the manger. This is what Christmas is all about."

Sal straighten his back and sighed. "I hate to throw in a wet towel, but we need to go across the street and tell Jerry about his new addition."

Maria turned toward the house, "I have a plate of Christmas cookies we can take to him. I'll get them and meet you both in the car."

Patty squinted and held her head with both hands. "Can I stay here?"

Sal took one of her hands and led her to the car. "Come on," he laughed. "I won't let him bite you."

As they pulled in the driveway, a man driving a gator approached them. There were grain cans and hay bales in the back of the gator.

Patty whispered. "That's the mean guy."

The man drove the gator up to their car. "Merry Christmas,"

he said smiling. Then he noticed Patty in the back seat and nodded to her. "I hope I didn't scare you off the other day."

The man tipped his black cowboy hat, then extended his hand to Sal. "I'm Tim, the foreman. Can I help you with something?"

Sal grinned and turned to look at Patty who was wide eyed and half smiling in the back seat. Then he gave Tim the news of the new birth.

"Go up to the house and tell Jerry," he said pointing to the little ranch house. "I'm sure he will appreciate meeting you." Then a sheepish grin formed under his mustache and he looked at Patty. "Jerry was concerned when I told him you ran off scared to death. I'm so sorry; I really didn't mean to scare you."

Maria and Sal turned around and chuckled at their daughter. Her face turned red with embarrassment. Then she looked at Tim who was smiling at her, and she burst into laughter.

Tim stood up straight and glanced at the house, "There's Jerry now." He waved to someone and hollered, "Merry Christmas, Jerry!"

An older man stood on the porch wearing pajamas and an old tattered bathrobe. He was average height, but broad in stature. His thick white hair covered his ears and part of his wire rim glasses, framing his warm jolly smile.

"Who do we have here?" Jerry beckoned.

"These folks have some news for you," Tim hollered to him, then nodded to Sal. "Go over and meet him."

Tim opened the back door of the car for Patty and whispered to her, "He doesn't bite either." Patty giggled and ran toward the porch.

"One of your donkeys had a baby in our Nativity Scene!" Patty anxiously blurted out.

Then Sal and Maria came up behind their daughter, introduced themselves, and gave news of the birth.

Jerry was silent and stared at them with a broad smile, sharing in their joy.

Upon Jerry's lack of words, Maria stuttered then extended her hand with the plate of cookies. "Merry Christmas, fresh baked cookies from our house to yours!"

Jerry stared at the cookies wrapped in red cellophane with a Christmas ribbon. "This is a Christmas surprise," he said chocking on his words. "New baby donkey, new neighbors, and a wonderful plate of fresh baked cookies."

Sal looked past him through the open front door of the house. There was no Christmas tree, decorations, or presents. "What are you doing for the rest of the day?"

"No plans," Jerry smiled looking at the ground. "I guess I should go with Tim to bring Mamma and baby home. I'll need to do that soon so he can go home with his family."

"You don't need to do that today," Maria chimed in. "We have provisions at our place. There's no reason to take Tim from his family." Maria bit her bottom lip, then continued. "Plus we are enjoying her."

"That's what I thought," Jerry chuckled.

"We would love for you to come to our house for dinner," Sal anxiously cut in. "We have a big turkey with stuffing, sweet potatoes, lasagna and pies for desert."

As Sal was talking, Jerry's smile widened and his eyes filled with tears. "I'd like that very much." Turning his head trying to hide his wet eyes, he pulled himself together and asked, "What time should I be there?"

"We'll eat around 4:00," Sal answered. "But come as early as you want."

"Come and see our new baby," Patty blurted then corrected herself and whispered. "I mean your new baby."

Jerry chuckled and extended his hand to Sal, Maria, then Patty. "I'll be over in a little while."

As Jerry was heading back to the house, Tim drove up along side of them in his black pick-up truck. "You must have said something that put a little pep in his step."

They all turned and watched Jerry dance across the porch. "Oh Christmas tree, Oh Christmas tree," he sang as he entered his house.

"Well, he's happy today," Tim laughed while lighting up a cigarette. He took a puff, then tipped his cowboy hat in farewell. "Ya all have a Merry Christmas."

Jerry set the plate of Christmas cookies on his dinning room table, then stepped back and stared at it. The Christmas colors gave the whole room a new appearance. He slipped his fingers under the wrapping and pulled out a chocolate chip cookie. He closed his eyes and smelled it, then giggled and took two more. He ate the cookies as he stared out the window at his donkeys. Two cardinals landed on the back of his favorite donkey. He often heard that the appearance of a cardinal is a sign that a deceased loved one is close by. He never gave it much thought until now. His eyes filled with tears and he whispered, "Merry Christmas." For the first time in many years, Jerry went to his computer and turned on Christmas music, then went to his room to change his clothes.

"Dinner's ready!" Sal beckoned everyone to the dinner table. Jerry slowly pulled out his chair as he looked around the room with a huge smile. When everyone was seated, Sal made the sign of the cross and began the blessing with his head bowed and his eyes closed. Maria and Patty did the same.

Jerry swallowed as a lump formed in his throat. He bowed his head and stared at the Advent Wreath in the middle of the table. The candles and greens were woven into a beautiful circle. Now, at this Christmas, his new neighbors were about to become his new circle. A tear fell from his eye, warming his cheek and warming his heart. He quickly wiped the tear before anyone could see.

After the food was passed around, Jerry asked, "So what brings you folks from New Jersey to Texas?"

"This was my grandfather's farm," Maria answered.

Sal then gave a brief account of what happened to their restaurant in the inner city and how he was trying to start a new life in Texas.

"I need to find a job," Sal chuckled.

Jerry put his fork down, wiped his mouth with the cloth Christmas napkin and gazed at the spread of food on the table. He took a deep breath before speaking.

"Have you been to Nonnie's Kitchen? It's a restaurant in downtown Magnolia."

Sal looked at Maria then answered, "No, we haven't been there."

Jerry leaned forward while focusing on Sal. His tone became serious. "The owner, Joseph Dassiano is a friend of mine. He's retiring and wants to sell the business. I am up for a new adventure,," Jerry paused. "Sooo, if I bought it, would you be interested in running it?"

"Say, 'Yes', Daddy," Patty giggled.

Sal, Maria and Patty looked at each other. Maria put her hand over her eyes to hide the tears. Sal's face lit up. He shook his head up and down without saying a word.

Sharing in their joy, Jerry added. "You are an excellent cook! There's no doubt about that!"

Then Jerry looked at Maria and Patty, "I am also looking for help with the donkeys. A couple of the donkeys know how to pull a cart and I would like to do some showing. I have carts and harnesses but no one to drive. Would you ladies be interested or would you prefer to help at the restaurant?"

"This is too good to be true," Patty's eyes burned with tears. "Mom knows all about driving donkeys." She pointed to the trophies on the mantle, then picked up Snickers who was waiting under her chair. "Suddenly we don't feel so homesick anymore! Do we Snickers?"

After dinner, they sat around the Christmas tree while Maria and Jerry shared donkey stories.

At midnight, Jerry stood up to say good-bye. "It's been a wonderful evening." His voice chocked, "Welcome to Texas."

"I'll be over tomorrow," Patty announced as she took a step toward him with Snickers in her arms.

"I'm looking forward to it." Jerry smiled warmly then turned to Maria and Sal. "Thank you again for this wonderful evening." Jerry opened the back door, then looked back at the family, "Merry Christmas and good night."

Patty stood at the window and watched Jerry walk to his car. Maria and Sal peered over her shoulder. Just before opening the car door, Jerry did a little dance, then turned and looked at the house again before getting in his car and driving off.

"Wonderful things happened today," Maria exclaimed. "And it all began with a New Life in the manger."

Christmas Homecoming

"It's about time," Andy Jo sighed as her father turned into the driveway with the horse trailer. He was an hour late returning from the fox hunt.

He slowed up when he saw her approaching and rolled the window down. "Andrea Josephine, hurry up. I have a surprise for you!"

A retired hound was the first thought that came to her mind. They had three dogs already, but taking in a retired fox hound would be an honor.

Andy Jo picked up her pace, but then slowed up when she saw a wooden cart in the back of the pickup truck.

She studied it for a second, then questioned her father. "Isn't that Mrs. Macklin's donkey cart?"

"It sure is," her father answered. "And inside the trailer, is Christopher, Mrs. Macklin's famous hilltop donkey."

"Hilltop," is a term used when one follows a fox hunt from a distance. Since Mrs. Geri Macklin was in her seventies, she felt more comfortable Hilltopping in the donkey cart. Galloping with a herd of horses, was now part of her past.

"So how did we end up with Christopher?" Andy Jo bit her lip as she lowered the trailer ramp.

I asked Geri if we could borrow Christopher for the live

Nativity scene at church. I was very surprised when she told me she was moving to FL and looking for a home for him.

"Okay….," Andy Jo responded as she held the donkey on the lead line and inspected him.

She knew Mrs. Macklin always took excellent care of her animals. Christopher's light gray coat was soft and thick. The black cross line over his shoulders was well pronounced as were the black stripes around his four legs. She knew the kids at the barn would love him, but how would he fit into her lesson program?

"Dad," she mumbled scratching her head. "I'm not sure I need another lesson pony, but we could use him when we go Christmas caroling tomorrow afternoon. One of the older students can drive the cart and at least two kids can ride along."

"That's a good idea," her father looked back at her as he lead his mule, Shindig, into the barn. "Just remember he needs to be at the church by 4:30 on Christmas Eve, the day after tomorrow."

It was two days before Christmas and the barn at 'A J Sebastian Stables' was filled with the hustle and bustle of Christmas Carolers.

After the wagons were decorated with holly and garlands, the students were divided into groups to observe the harnessing of the three animals that would be pulling them.

Andy Jo harnessed the big mule, Shindig, and her best friend Joanne, harnessed the molly, Mary Lou. One of the older students, Buffy, took charge of harnessing Christopher.

Andy Jo took pride in knowing that teaching kids how to harness, was something that most lesson barns didn't offer. She loved the kids in her lesson program, and they loved her.

"Now everyone needs to step back," she commanded as she led Shindig out of the barn to be hooked up to the wagon.

She nodded to Buffy, "Please hold him while Joanne and I get the wagon."

The children watched intently as the shafts were put through the tugs and the tracers fastened to the wagon.

"Can I ride up front in the big wagon with you?" Lizzie whispered to Andy Jo.

"Of course," she whispered back. Lizzie giggled and gently clapped her hands together.

When all three animals were harnessed and hitched, the little caravan began their adventure. Their caroling route had been plotted around a neighborhood not far from the stables.

"This used to be a huge cow farm," Andy Jo informed Lizzie. "It was sold to developers when I was a little girl." Then she pointed in a direction behind the development. "We will pass by the original farm house at the end of the development. I'm not sure if anyone lives there now."

Lizzie only nodded as she focused on the huge blow up Santa at a nearby house. Shindig stopped dead in his tracks and brayed at the monster. Mary Lou and Christopher followed suit.

There were two boys playing basketball at the house next to the Santa. They stopped what they were doing when they heard Shindig's bray.

"What was that?" One of the boys shouted, as the other boy stepped back.

Robin, one of the carolers, recognized the boy from school and stood up with her hands on her hips. "That was Shindig braying at the big Santa."

"Now what?" Joanne called from the wagon behind her.

Andy Jo turned to Robin, "Do you know this boy?"

"His name is Aiden," Robin proudly responded.

"Hello Aiden," Andy Jo called from the wagon.

"Hello," the boy quietly responded and put his head down.

"Could you please do me a big favor?"

As Aiden began to step toward the wagons, a gentle wind blew the inflated Santa and Shindig let out a loud snort.

"Whoa!" Aiden jumped back.

The children in the wagons burst into laughter.

"He won't hurt you, I promise," Andy Jo chuckled. "Please go over to that big blow up Santa and put your hand on it."

Aiden hesitated.

"It's okay," Andy Jo encouraged. "If Shindig sees you touching it, he will know it is harmless."

"Just go touch it," one of the children shouted from Shindig's wagon.

Keeping an eye on the mule, Aiden slowly walked to the Santa and gently touched it.

The big mule watched with wide eyes before smacking his lips in submission. Then he nodded his head and stepped forward. Knowing the coast was clear, Mary Lou and Christopher followed.

As this was happening, Aiden's father came out of the house to see what was going on. He started to speak, but then turned and called his wife to the door.

"Hi there!" Aiden's mother called from the porch. "What's going on?"

"We are about to sing some Christmas Carols for you," Katerina spoke up from Mary Lou's wagon.

The woman motioned with her hand for the wagons to

come closer to the house. When all three wagons were lined up, Katerina opened up in song and the rest of the carolers joined in.

Their sweet angelic voices carried through the crisp air to the nearby neighbors.

Front doors opened and people came out of their houses to listen to the children. Some treated them to cookies and some treated the animals with carrots and apples.

"That was so much fun!" Joanne shouted as they drove away from the last house.

"My throat is starting to get sore," Robin laughed. "It's a good thing we are finished."

"I'm not so sure about that," Andy Jo pointed to an elderly woman standing by an old rusty gate at the end of the road.

"I think someone is now living in that old farm house," she mumbled.

The woman stepped out of the gate as the wagons approached. She didn't speak, but smiled and waved to the children. When the wagons came to a stop, she stepped into the road and walked toward Christopher.

"Hello Pretty Fellow," she greeted the donkey, then smiled at Buffy and the two students in the cart.

"May I?" she nodded as she took a carrot out of her pocket and motioned toward Christopher.

As Christopher took the carrot from her hand, she touched his ears with the other hand, oblivious of the wagons and carolers.

AJ turned Shindig around and walked toward the woman. "Hi there, would you like to hear a Christmas carol?"

The woman looked at AJ and giggled. "Sure, as long as I can keep petting this beautiful creature."

The kids broke into song as the elderly woman caressed

Christopher's ears. The donkey took a step closer to the woman and pressed his head into her chest. She smiled radiantly and put both arms around his head.

When the song finished, she stepped back and looked into the donkey's eyes. "I think this donkey likes me!"

Andy Jo cleared her throat. "Excuse me, ma'am, I hope you enjoyed our song." There was a pause and Andy Jo spoke again. "We are from the riding stables down the road. My name is Andy Jo."

The woman glanced at Andy Jo then stepped back to the curb.

"My name is Hannah," the woman smiled sweetly. "I hope you will bring this donkey back to see me again."

"It is nice meeting you, Hannah. We will come back another day, I promise. We must be on our way, as it will be getting dark soon."

"Okay, goodbye." Hannah smiled and waved. "I'm looking forward to seeing you again!" She stepped back through the rusty gate and waved again as the caravan drove away.

Andy Jo's spine stiffened as she led the small caravan down the road. She kept her eyes forward as if she was afraid to look back.

"Are you sad about that old woman?" Lizzie put her hand on Andy Jo's arm.

Andy Jo tried to answer but a lump in her throat prevented her from getting the words out. She swallowed hard then responded.

"That was sad. I need to do something for her. After all, it is Christmas!"

"I hope Santa comes to her house," Lizzie gave her arm a little squeeze.

The next morning at the breakfast table, Andy Jo's mother

put her hand on Andy Jo's shoulder. "You are awfully quiet this morning."

Andy Jo sighed, then took a sip of her coffee.

Her mother continued. "I thought you would be more in the Christmas sprit after your caroling adventure yesterday."

"It was a lot of fun," she confessed. "But just as we were leaving the development, an elderly woman came out of the old farm house and made a fuss over Christopher."

"And ….." Her mother beckoned for her to continue.

"She said her name was Hannah." Andy Jo took a deep breath, "She appeared very lonely".

"Do you mean Hannah Johnson from the dairy farm?" Andy Jo's father cut in?

"She didn't say her last name." Andy Jo put her coffee cup down with a thud.

"Yesterday when I was at the deli, old Amos Myers said Hannah is back in town."

Andy Jo sat up a straighter, her eyes beamed at her father. "Someone knows her?"

"Amos went to school with Hannah. He remembers she used to drive a donkey cart to deliver milk to the neighbors."

"That's why she was so happy to see Christopher." Andy Jo sighed.

"Amos said Hannah loved that donkey." Her father smiled and shook his head. "If you don't think you can use Christopher as a lesson donkey, maybe you could give him to Hannah. Of course, that is if she has the provisions and if she is up to it."

"Dad, that's a great idea!" Andy Jo stood up and gave her father a hug. "The yard is fenced in and I saw a little barn out back."

"Make sure the fence and barn are in good condition," her

mother piped in. "We promised Mrs. Macklin we would take care of Christopher."

"We also promised Father Mike a donkey for the live nativity scene this evening and we have a lot to do today. We can talk to Hannah later."

"Okay," she sighed. "We can talk to Hannah later." She slowly put on her coat and walked to the barn.

The family drove to Christmas Eve mass in the pick up truck with the horse trailer and donkey in tow. Andy Jo couldn't get the old woman out of her mind. "I hope she comes to the service tonight. She'll be so happy to see Christopher."

They pulled into the church parking lot next to O'Shea's Sheep Farm trailer. Two members of the youth group were leading lambs to the Nativity stable.

People began lining up along the sidewalk to get a closer look as the live Nativity Scene began to unfold.

Dressed in her Sunday coat and hat, Andy Jo scanned the crowd as she lead Christopher to the stable.

She didn't see Hannah, but Andy Jo wasn't giving up hope. She left Christopher with the O'Shea family who was managing the Nativity scene.

Christmas mass was as beautiful as always, but Andy Jo's thoughts kept flashing back to Hannah, all alone, waving to the carolers and the donkey.

"Andrea Josephine," her father called to her after the last hymn. "Where are you going?"

"I have to…" Was all she could say before someone interrupted and shook her father's hand, wishing him a Merry Christmas. The crowd had thickened between her and her parents, as she continued toward the Nativity Scene in hopes of seeing Hannah.

The stable had already drawn a remarkable crowd, as people lined the sidewalk. Cameras flashed and some spectators treated the animals with carrots and apples.

Andy Jo smiled to herself knowing that if Hannah were present, she would have a special treat for the donkey.

She stood on the steps in silence. Her eyes scanned the crowd for Hannah. "Wishful thinking," she thought to herself and walked back to the truck and trailer where her parents were waiting for her.

"Where have you been?" Her father asked raising his eyebrows.

"I... I was going to check on Christopher, but there's a slew of people there." Andy Jo forced a chuckle. "I guess most of those people haven't seen farm animals before."

Andy Jo's mother sensed her dismay and put her hand on her shoulder. "Honey, what's wrong?"

"Oh nothing," Andy Jo sighed.

"Were you looking for Hannah?" her mother leaned closer to her.

"Yeah," Andy Jo frowned.

Her mother offered no words of comfort, but gave her arm a little squeeze.

Her father started up the truck. "We have some time before they are finished with Christopher. Let's get something at Dunkin Donuts."

"Sounds like a plan," Andy Jo forced a smile.

Andy Jo's mood changed from gloom to Christmas spirit as they drove out of the parking lot with Christmas Carols playing on the radio. They discussed the hustle and bustle that would take place the next day as Andy Jo ate the whipped cream from the top of her hot chocolate. The minutes flew by as the early evening turned to night.

"I guess it is time to pack it in," her father chuckled as he waved to Father Mike who was trying to lead one of the lambs to the trailer. Father's smile was radiant as he challenged the little lamb to go home.

"I'm sure he misses all of this from growing up on a sheep farm in Ireland," Andy Jo's mother rolled down the window and waved.

Andy Jo stretched her neck to get a glimpse but then her eye caught sight of an old woman standing near the donkey.

"It's Hannah!" She blurted out.

"Where?" Her mother asked.

Before Andy Jo could answer, her father turned the truck around to maneuver into a parking spot. When the truck came to a stop, Andy Jo lost sight of the old woman.

On Christmas morning Hannah woke up wearing a smile. Just the memory of seeing the donkey the night before made the holiday special.

She had only been home for a week and hadn't taken the time to explore her new surroundings and make new friends. She spent every minute cleaning her house that had been vacant for several years since her parents' death. She lived in California for forty years until she recently became a widow.

Now she was all alone. She looked out the window at her old stable. Memories of King James, her little donkey, crossed her mind. She remembered delivering cookies along with milk to all of her neighbors on Christmas mornings.

Sitting around feeling sorry for herself, was not something

she would allow herself to do. "I'm going to bake some cookies," she said out loud. "And I know just where to deliver them."

Hannah giggled to herself as she put the cookie ingredients on the table.

Early that morning, Andy Jo and her dog Sam walked back to the house after feeding the animals their breakfast. She mixed a little molasses with a carrot and an apple into each food bucket as a Christmas treat.

Her parents were still sleeping and the house was quiet. She tiptoed around the living room, turning on the Christmas tree lights and the lights on the mantle.

She laughed to herself remembering that, a few short years ago, she was still a teenager, and Joey, her older brother was still living at home. She was not allowed to come downstairs on Christmas morning until all the Christmas lights were turned on. It was part of the Santa spirit. Now, she was playing Santa spirit and turning the lights on for her parents. Her brother Joey was doing the same thing for his wife and two children at their house. She was anxious to see them later in the day.

She put the cinnamon biscuits in the oven and said to Sam, "Maybe the aroma of the biscuits will wake them." Sam licked his lips as if he knew she was talking about food.

Then she poured herself a cup of coffee and opened the pantry door to get a cookie for Sam. The sleigh bells hanging on the door with a red bow jingled and caught her off guard.

"Sleigh bells," she chuckled, then gave Sam a couple of cookies. "Maybe that will wake them."

Although the bells were authentic, they were only used as a Christmas decoration. She ran her hand down the leather strap that held the bells. "I could have used these the other day when we went caroling."

She sat at the kitchen table with her coffee and peered out the window. Sam sat next to her with his head on her lap. "It's starting to snow," she said to her dog. "I guess it will be a white Christmas after all."

She feasted her eyes on the Christmas tree and the presents underneath. A pink tricycle tucked in a big Christmas bag stood next to the tree. Andy Jo felt a wave of excitement as she pictured her little niece opening the bag. In the back of the tree, a few presents were wrapped for 'just in case.' Mom always bought some extra things from Avon for just in case anyone unexpected happened to stop in.

"I wish Hannah would stop in," she said to Sam caressing his ears.

"Why don't you invite her?" Mom's voice responded as she came down the stairs.

"Are you serious?" Andy Jo jumped out of the chair.

"Yes, I'm serious." Her mother said as she poured herself a cup of coffee. "The neighborhood has changed since she's been gone. She doesn't have any family left. Let's give her a homecoming Christmas."

"Thank's Mom!" Andy Jo gave her mother a big hug.

"Are the biscuits ready?" Her father walked in the room and noticed the excitement in his daughter's eyes. "What's going on?"

"I am picking Hannah up in the donkey cart." Andy Jo shouted with joy as she put on her coat and headed toward the backdoor.

"What?" Her father responded scratching his head.

Andy Jo walked back to the pantry door, removed the sleigh

bells and jingled them. "Sleigh bells ring, are you listening…" she sang, then left the house for the barn.

A few minutes later sleigh bells jingled as Christopher trotted down the road toward Hannah's house with a red bow on his head. Her parents ran to the picture window and waved to her. She waved back and hollered, "Merry Christmas."

The snowflakes were gently falling, but not sticking to the pavement. Christopher kept up his pace as if he knew the importance of this mission. Hannah's house was a little over a mile down the road. That would be no problem for a donkey who was a seasoned hill topper.

Hannah put her coat on and walked outside to get the newspaper. As snow flakes landed on her head, a wave of uncertainty fell upon her. "I can't go anywhere if it is snowing." After living in California for so many hears, she had forgotten how to drive in the snow. The snow hadn't begun to stick to the roads, but when it did, she would be in trouble. "I guess I am not going anywhere today," she sighed. "I wish I had someone to spend the day with."

Hannah's house came into view and Andy Jo prayed that the sound of the sleigh bells would carry to Hannah through the crisp morning snow fall.

"Hurry," she tapped the reins on Christopher's back. "I think I see her."

As Andy Jo studied the scene. Hannah was picking up the morning newspaper. As they got closer, Andy Jo knew Hannah noticed them.

"Hannah!" Andy Jo waved and Christopher trotted faster.

The woman pulled her coat tighter across her chest with one hand and waved excitedly with the other hand.

"Merry Christmas," Andy Jo greeted her.

Before Christopher came to a stop, Hannah ran through the gate to greet the donkey.

Framing the bow with her hands, she cried "I am so happy to see you. Can you stay for a visit?"

"Well actually I have come to pick you up."

"Oh?" Hannah tilted her head.

"Yeah," Andy Jo patted the bench seat in the cart. "Hop in. We would love for you to spend Christmas Day at our house."

A silence fell between the two women. Hannah closed her eyes and whispered, "Thank you Baby Jesus."

"Let me get some warmer clothes." She shivered then hurried back through the gate to the house.

Within a few short minutes, she came out of the house carrying a basket of cookies.

"These are fresh out of the oven," Hannah smiled as she climbed into the cart.

The snow continued to fall as Christopher trotted toward home.

The sleigh bells jiggled as Hannah shared stories of her donkey, King James, and Christmases of long ago.

"When I get settled, I plan on getting another donkey. I miss driving all over town and seeing the neighbors."

"I don't know about driving all over town in this day and age, but from my house to your house you are safe." She handed Hannah the reins. "Here is your donkey. He can stay with us until you get settled."

Tears ran down Hannah's face as she took the reins from her new young friend.

"Happy Birthday Baby Jesus," Hannah shouted. "And Merry Christmas to all."

The Barnyard Nativity

"This is no way to get time off!" Troy chuckled at his buddy, Michael, lying in the hospital bed with his leg in a cast.

Michael chuckled back as he raised the bed to siting position. "This is no time off, believe me. They give me quite a work out in physical therapy."

"I had no idea you were here until the Knights of Columbus' meeting last night." Troy removed his cap, unbuttoned his coat, then sat down. "Keith said he picked you up in the ambulance last week. I don't know why he didn't make it known."

Michael shook his head. "He turned on the sirens and the red flashing lights as if it were some big medical emergency!"

Troy raised his eyebrows. "Michael, at our age, a fall is an emergency."

Michael took a deep breath and put his hands under his casted leg. "I know, but the lights and sirens scared my animals." He shook his head and thought for a moment.

"My son asked his neighbor, Chelsea, to care for his broodmares while he and his family are in Connecticut. I assume he asked her to take care of my animals as well." Michael shrugged his shoulders. "They'll be back tomorrow, but will you stop at my farm and check on them?"

"Of course." Troy stood and squeezed Michael's shoulder. "I'm happy to do that."

"I have been here for ten days already," Michael tapped his cast. "They are sending me home tomorrow morning."

"Call me when you get released and I'll pick you up." Troy grinned mischievously. "You know tomorrow is Christmas Eve. We are setting up the Nativity stable, then the kids are having a dress rehearsal for their Christmas pageant. Are you up to going?"

"I'll supervise from the wheel chair!" His bright smile shined like a Christmas star. "How many animals are we hosting this year? Are we getting the camel?"

Troy frowned. "The animals aren't coming this year." He paused, then buttoned his coat. "I assume someone out bid us and got the camel and all the other animals." He shook his head. "The little girl who is playing Mary in the pageant is heart broken."

Troy took a deep breath as he twirled his wool cap in his hand. "My wife's donkey, Christopher, has an abscess and my donkey, Crystal, has never been ridden. I feel helpless."

Michael grabbed the bed rail and pulled himself up taller. "My donkey Squeaky Wheels, is available. My grandchildren ride her and she is used to parades and crowds!"

Troy smiled with relief. "I am sure the kids will be happy to hear that; especially Lizzie. Too bad you don't have any sheep or a camel," Troy chuckled.

"They can pretend the goats are sheep and the pig is a camel," Michael chuckled back at him.

Thirty minutes later, Troy drove into Michael's driveway, stretching his neck in search of the donkey, two goats, and a pot belly pig. Instead he found a teenage girl throwing hay over the fence to the brood mares.

"Hi there," he called to her. "I'm Troy, Michael's friend. I came to check on his animals. You must be Chelsea."

The girl stood with her mouth opened for a few seconds before answering. "Michael's car is here. So I guess he's in the house."

Troy looked around the field where the animals should have been and noticed the fence was down. "No he's not here," Troy spoke softly. "He's been in the hospital for the last ten days." He pointed to the broken fence. "It looks like the animals have gotten out."

Chelsea's face reddened as she held back the tears. "No one told me anything about Michael in the hospital! His animals were here yesterday, I know they were!" She looked around the fields, then at Troy. "There was some hay on the ground from the round bale and I never thought to check the water because Michael always does that."

Troy gave her shoulder a squeeze and bent down to look into her eyes. "This isn't your fault. If the animals were starving or dying of thirst, you would have noticed something. We'll find them."

Troy and Chelsea walked through the field toward the broken fence. "It looks like they broke out to get to the stream," Troy pointed to the hoof prints.

"Squeaky Wheels! Popcorn! Peanuts! Pavarotti!" Chelsea bellowed out as she peered through the woods searching for the little herd.

"I assume the goats are Popcorn and Peanuts," Troy chuckled

as he tried to humor Chelsea. "Aren't they wearing bells around their neck?"

"Yeah," Chelsea looked up at him. "If they aren't too far off, we should be able to hear them."

"Let's separate for a few minutes and keep in touch with our phones," Troy advised.

Troy walked briskly with his eyes wide open, searching for the small herd. Off in a distance, Chelsea called for each animal by name, pleading for their return. When he saw a car passing by, he knew he had reached the road. He took out his cell and called Chelsea.

"Did you find them?" She answered with excitement.

"No, Sweetie," Troy paused. "I'll notify the police, then we should drive around the neighborhood in separate cars and look for them."

They spent the next three hours driving around, then ended their search for the night.

Not far from Michael's farm, the four animals rummaged through a corn field searching for anything the corn picker may have left behind. When they grew tired, they decided it was time to head back home, with Pavarotti leading the way. They almost reached the road, when a police car drove by with red flashing lights. The animals stopped and huddled together. They remembered the red flashing lights the night Michael was carried away. The donkey tossed her head, signaling to the other three to follow.

Popcorn, Peanuts, and Pavarotti followed single file through a field, that connected to the baseball complex.

Pavarotti sniffed all the empty garbage cans hoping to find something to eat. Popcorn munched on an ice cream wrapper.

Peanuts checked out the ice tub and was happy to find it filled with water. All four animals drank their fill, then curled up under the bleachers and fell asleep.

The herd woke up at the break of dawn and looked to their donkey leader. Squeaky Wheels remembered giving rides to kids at the church bazaar. She remembered there was plenty of food and she remembered how to get there. She tossed her head and signaled for the goats and pig to follow.

Sarah Duncan took her last two Christmas pies out of the oven while her husband and children were still asleep. She tiptoed around the kitchen and wondered if the pie aroma would wake them. "I'll set the pies outside on the deck to cool off where the aroma won't reach anyone."

After she put the pies down on a bench, she smiled at the string popcorn and pinecones smeared with peanut butter and birdseed that her children had put out for the birds' Christmas.

"Burr," she giggled as she rubbed her arms and quickly stepped back in the warm house. She picked up her laundry basket and went to the basement.

Pavarotti squealed as he jumped out of line and galloped toward the aroma of Sarah's Christmas pies. The goats and the donkey followed him without thinking twice. Two minutes later, the four animals landed on Sarah's deck and feasted on her pies and bird treats that her children made.

As Sarah was walking up from the basement, she heard bells, that didn't sound like Christmas bells. Her four year old son was looking out the window and laughing. "Goats are eating the pine cones and popcorn!"

"What?" She screeched, dropped the laundry basket and ran to the window. She didn't know if she should laugh or cry. The goats were licking peanut butter from their lips, while the pig's face was covered with pumpkin pie. The donkey looked straight at her, then brayed to the other three animals. The donkey lead the way, as the four animals jumped down from the deck and ran back to the fields.

The telephone rang and woke Troy from a sound sleep. "Hey Troy," a voice chuckled from the other end. "It's Lieutenant Falcon. Your animals were spotted in Keith Duncan's yard early this morning."

Troy jumped out of bed. "Are they okay?"

"Keith's wife said they were on her deck and ate two of her pies!" Lieutenant laughed. "His kid said the goats ate the decorations they put out for the birds." Lieutenant continued laughing. "They know where to find good food."

Troy chuckled. "Thank you for calling me. I'm glad they are okay."

Troy drove around the neighborhood with his horse trailer searching for the herd.

His cell phone rang. He squinted when he read Michael's name on the caller ID. He wasn't sure how he would break the news to his friend.

A nurse's aid helped Michael into Troy's truck. After he settled into his seat, his smile fell as he noticed a look of dismay on Troy's face.

"What's going on?" Michael turned and nodded toward the horse trailer.

Troy swallowed, then cleared his throat. "Your animals got out last night. I have been driving around looking for them."

Michael's jaw dropped. "What?"

Troy put his hand on Michael's shoulder. "They were spotted early this morning on Keith Duncan's deck feasting on his wife's Christmas pies."

Michael looked out the window and scratched his head. He faced Troy for a second, then burst into laughter. "Her pies are the best! Pavarotti must have sniffed them out!"

"They can't be too far. I brought bags of carrots and apples to lure them." He handed a bag to Michael, then looked at his watch. "We have time to drive around one more time." Troy pointed to the back of his truck. "Then I need to deliver this hay to the church for the Nativity stable."

Michael slipped the carrots into his coat pocket. His eyes widened as he scanned through the window for his little herd.

"I didn't have a chance to mention to anyone about using your animals," Troy informed Michael as he drove into the church parking lot.

Michael faced him then firmly stated. "I am sure we will find them."

The Nativity stable was almost completed. Aaron, one of the knights, was installing electric cords for the plastic light up sheep and camels that would take the place of the live animals.

Standing next to the Nativity stable, was Lizzie dressed in a Mary costume her mother made for her. She held a Baby Jesus doll as tears rolled down her chubby cheeks. Troy closed his eyes and rubbed his forehead. A feeling of dread came over him, as if the animals' absence was his fault.

Troy's buddy, Carmen, waved then beckoned to Aaron. The two men anxiously approached the truck. Michael gave Troy a big smile, then rolled his window down and extended his arm.

Carmen took a hold of his hand and chuckled. "You're late! We are almost finished."

Aaron nodded to Michael and Troy, then lifted the hay bale out of the truck bed. "Are there more hay bales in the trailer?"

"No," Troy sighed. "We have been driving around looking for Michael's animals."

"The ones that ate Keith's wife's pies?" Aaron chuckled, then turned his head toward the sound of clanging bells. He dropped the hay bale and pointed to the driveway entrance. "Here comes the culprits now!"

Troy caught sight of the animals approaching from his side view mirror and shouted. "They're here!"

Michael had been engaged in a conversation with Carmen. He looked dumfound at Troy. "Who's here?"

"Your donkey, goats and pig," Troy fumbled as he unfastened his seat belt.

The herd walked nonchalantly toward the truck and trailer. The donkey caught sight of Michael leaning out the window and trotted to him.

"Squeaker," Michael pulled a carrot from his coat pocket and handed it to the donkey. The goats and pig hurried to the truck and demanded their share. "I was getting worried about you kids." Michael rubbed Squeaker's long ears then opened the truck door.

As Carmen and Troy were helping Michael into the wheel chair, the herd caught everyone's attention.

Lizzie jogged across the parking lot, carrying her Baby Jesus doll with one hand and holding up her long dress with the other hand. The rest of the children dressed in their pageant costumes followed her.

Michael put his hand up. "Kids don't run toward the animals. We don't want to scare them."

"Mr. Michael, is this your donkey? Did he come here for me to ride in the Christmas pageant?"

"I believe so," Michael's voice chocked as he put his hand on the donkey's neck, then whistled for the other three animals to follow him into the stable.

Troy pushed the wheel chair, while Aaron carried the hay bale, and Carmen walked behind the herd keeping them together. The children giggled as they walked behind Carmen.

"I thought we ordered two sheep and a camel!" One of the parents joked. 'Is this their replacement? Two goats and a pig?"

"This will have to do," Michael chucked back.

The goats and donkey munched on the hay in the manger while the pig wandered around begging for handouts.

"Awwe! There's evidence smeared all over Pavarotti's face," Troy laughed as he held the pig's face with both hands. "You were eating Sarah's pumpkin pie, weren't you?"

Troy beckoned to the children, "Keep these critters occupied, while I get some supplies from the trailer." Then he spoke to Aaron, "Can you bring the hose around?"

Troy returned from the trailer carrying buckets, Pavarotti's harness, a halter, and lead lines. Lizzie graciously took the halter and a lead line from Troy's hand.

"I know about donkeys and horses," she proudly remarked to the rest of the children. She put the halter on the donkey then led her to the water bucket. The other animals also drank.

Troy put the harness on Pavarotti and held him while

Aaron washed his face. The pig let out a painful squeal and tried unsuccessfully to squirm away from Troy. Everyone stopped what they were doing and looked on with horror.

"You are hurting him!" One little girl cried.

"He's okay," Michael reassured the child. "He's just singing." Michael saw the little girl looking back at him with disbelief. "That's why we named him 'Pavarotti.' He loves to sing."

"Is everyone ready for dress rehearsal?" Mr. Flynn, the director spoke.

Lizzie handed the lead line to Joseph, who was playing Joseph in the pageant, then Troy lifted her onto the donkey's back.

"You're supposed to sit sideways if you are playing Mary," Joseph scolded her.

"I don't know how to ride side ways. I only ride like this." Lizzie sat up tall with one leg on each side of the donkey.

All was going very well with the dress rehearsal. Mr. Flynn held the script tightly in both hands, and intently watched every movement, nodding his head with each line the children delivered. Michael, Aaron and Troy watched with wide eyes and open mouth as the children's angelic voices carried through the crisp afternoon air.

It was the last song before the closing song. Michelle and Faith took center stage twirling on their toes, then leaped in unison across the stage. As they twirled around a second time, the director bit his bottom lip in anticipation of their next move.

The angels ran across the stage and leaped high in the air, in a perfect unison with their legs and arms spread far apart. At the hight of their perfect jete', their wings became unfastened and floated in the air above the animals.

The goats panicked and raced out of the stable with the pig

squealing behind them. The director ordered the cast to keep still until the animals were under control.

Troy and Aaron ran after the animals and tackled them in the bushes. Michael wheeled his chair closer to Squeaker, and stroked her ears to keep her from getting excited. Squeaker was unfazed by the episode and nuzzled his pocket for treats.

"Give me a few minutes to put these three back in the trailer," Troy informed everyone as he drug both goats by the collar. Aaron followed with both hands on the pig's harness. The three animals jumped in the trailer and devoured the carrots and apples Troy had packed earlier.

"Well you know what they say," Michelle laughed as she retrieved her wings from the stable.

"Bad dress rehearsal, good performance," Faith responded. Both girls looked at each other and laughed.

"Let's hope so!" Mr. Flynn chuckled as he took the wings from the girls. "You certainly don't need these wings to perform that beautiful jete'!"

Troy took the animals home, then spent the next two hours reinforcing the Nativity stable so the animals couldn't escape.

When it was time, Troy and Michael returned to the church with the small herd. The animals settled quietly in the new stable.

"My Mamma put make-up on me," Lizzie blinked her eyes at Troy as he lifted her onto Squeaker's back. Her Mamma smiled at her and Troy as she adjusted Lizzie's costume around her chubby little legs.

"Are you both ready to take your place now?" Troy asked Lizzie and Jospeh?

Joseph took a deep breath, smiled brightly and gripped the lead line with both hands. "I am ready."

"What about you Lizzie?" Troy asked with a wide grin.

"I have been ready for this my whole life!" Lizzie sat up taller on the donkey's back and raised her chin.

The crowd fell silent as Aaron turned on the spot light and captured Joseph leading Mary on the donkey.

Michael's two grandchildren sat on each side of him. His granddaughter snuggled closer and whispered in his ear. "Poppi, I am proud of our donkey." Michael nodded, then put his finger to his lips.

Troy and his wife, Hannah sat behind Lizzie's parents. Tears fell from Lizzie's Mamma's eyes as she delivered her lines. Hannah gently rubbed her shoulder, then handed her a tissue.

The children's beautiful voices carried through the night air and filled the neighborhood. People coming out of a nearby church, stood on the sidewalk and basked in the serenade.

Mr. Flynn silently applauded and whispered, "Stupendous," as Michelle and Faith gracefully leaped in unison executing a perfect jete'.

At the closing scene, Joseph beckoned to the crowd to join the cast in singing Silent Night.

When the song was finished, total silence fell on the crowd.

Then Squeaky Wheels let out a loud bray, telling everyone Merry Christmas, good night, and it's time to go home.

Jeremiah And Starlight

Mary rubbed Jeremiah's long soft ears and whispered to him as she often did. The donkey closed his eyes, pressed his head to Mary's heart, and listened to every word.

"An angel came into my bedroom last night," Mary's voice grew more excited as she spoke. "He said his name was Gabriel. He was tall with long curly golden hair. He said I am to have a Son, and I am to name Him, Jesus. Gabriel said, He will be great and He will be called the Son of the Most High God."

Mary closed her eyes for a minute, then continued speaking. "Gabriel said the Holy Spirit will come upon me and the power of the Most High will cover me." Mary stepped back from the donkey and put her arms in the air and began to dance.

"I am the handmaid of the Lord. Let this happen to me. I can't wait to tell Joseph."

Mary's mother, Ann, was about to call her in for breakfast when she noticed Mary whispering to Jeremiah. Ann sighed and stared at her daughter. "She is so young," Ann thought as she rubbed her hands on her apron. "But, in a few short weeks, she and Jospeh will be married." Ann remembered Mary was only six years old when the donkey was born. He was smaller than the other donkeys. Mary looked after him and named him Jeremiah.

Mary believed one day this donkey would do something very important.

Mary's father, Joachim, walked toward the house, carrying two buckets of water he drew from the well. He stopped and put the buckets down and watched his daughter dance. He took a deep breath knowing God had called his daughter to do something very special. Even though she willingly said, "Yes," her calling wouldn't be easy. Joachim heard the soft bray of Joseph's mule, Starlight. He rubbed his chin and sighed deeply.

When Mary saw Joseph approaching, she stopped dancing and ran to him. Jeremiah jogged behind her.

Joachim watched as Joseph put his arms around Mary. Mary took his hand and lead him under the shade tree. Joachim watched his daughter put her hand on her stomach as she spoke to Joseph.

Joseph took a step back and stared at the ground. He slowly walked back to Starlight, mounted him, then rode away.

Jeremiah jogged to Mary. She stood under the tree staring after Joseph. Tears ran down her face. The donkey put his head on her shoulder, while Mary closed her eyes and prayed.

Unable to sleep that night, Joseph paced the floor and recited psalms asking for God's help. When his legs were too tired to pace anymore, he plopped on his bed and fell into a deep sleep.

An angel appeared to him in a dream and told him everything Mary said was true. The angel told Joseph to marry Mary and take care of the Child Jesus.

Joseph threw the covers back and jumped out of bed. "Mary!" He called out staring at a moonbeam on the wall. As he held his chest and panted, the shadow of his mule's head appeared in the moonbeam.

"Oh Starlight, did I wake you?" The mule yawned and blinked with his head through the open window.

"An angel came to me in a dream. How could I have doubted Mary?" Joseph covered his face with his hands and wept. The mule nuzzled Joseph's cheek, catching the warm tears that fell.

"I must go to her first thing in the morning." The mule continued to listen with his eyes closed. "I'll need you to take me," Joseph put his head close to the mule's big ear. "You can always make her laugh."

Early the next morning, Joseph mounted Starlight and set out for Mary's house. Out of habit, the mule stopped at a patch of wild flowers along the road. Joseph quickly jumped down and picked a bouquet, then hopped back on his mule and continued down the road.

Ann and Joachim were working in the garden as Joseph approached. Joachim put his hands on his hips and stared. Ann stepped closer to Joachim and put her arms around his arm.

Joseph bowed his head and held up the flowers. Joachim sighed with relief, then he and Ann bent down and continued working.

Jeremiah brayed and jogged to the house alerting Mary of Joseph's arrival. When Joseph saw her standing in the doorway, he urged Starlight to pick up his pace.

"Oh Mary," Joseph quickly jumped down from his mule. Before he could say another word, Starlight bowed his head and kissed Mary's belly.

"Your mule is smarter than you," Mary chuckled.

"Oh Mary," Joseph said again and handed her the flowers.

A few weeks later Joseph and Mary were married.

Joseph worked in his carpenter shop; crafting tables, chairs and other pieces of furniture. Mary loved to sew and embroider. She always sang psalms as she worked.

As the days went on and the seasons changed, Mary blossomed in her pregnancy. One morning as she and Joseph were finishing breakfast, Mary smiled at Joseph and put her hand to her belly. "The Baby is active this morning," she giggled. "It won't be much longer."

Joseph looked down at her belly, then smiled at her. "I hope He has your beautiful eyes." Then he gently squeezed her hand and left for his shop.

Mary raised her chin and smiled with admiration as she watched her husband leave. "God had been good to me," she whispered.

That afternoon as Jeremiah and Starlight grazed in the pasture, two strangers rode into town on horseback.

Everyone stopped what they were doing and stared. "This could be trouble," one neighbor whispered.

Jeremiah and Starlight knew something wasn't right. They looked at each other and jogged to the house. Jeremiah put his nose through the kitchen window, letting Mary know he was there.

Joseph stood in the doorway of his shop and put his hand on Starlight's neck. "They are King Herod's soldiers," Joseph whispered to his mule.

One of the men unrolled a paper and read, "This is an order

form Caesar Augustus. Everyone is to report to their place of birth to be counted." The soldiers looked around to make sure everyone was listening, then rode off.

Some of the people sighed with relief, but Joseph put his hand to his head and moaned. "My place of birth is Bethlehem, ninety miles away."

Starlight nuzzled his cheek. He gently grabbed the mules big ear and sighed. "Mary was so happy this morning; now I need to break this news to her."

"A caravan heading south along the Jordan will be leaving in the morning." Joseph informed Mary.

Mary looked up at Joseph and smiled brightly. Putting her hands on her belly, she replied. "We will be ready."

In those days, people traveled in caravans to protect themselves against thieves and wild animals. They either walked, or rode in carts or on top of donkeys, mules, or horses. The caravans traveled about ten miles a day. They stopped in towns where some travelers stayed and other travelers joined.

Joseph went back to his shop and put away the table he was making. He took another piece of wood, and began to fabricate wheels for a cart. Starlight watched from the doorway.

"Do you think you can pull this cart and carry me at the same time?" Joseph raised his eyebrows as he spoke to his mule.

The mule brayed softly in response. Joseph chuckled and gently grabbed his big ear.

Very early the next morning, Joseph packed the cart and helped Mary up on Jeremiah's back. He carefully folded blankets around her, then squeezed her hand. "We'll stop and say 'Good-bye' to your parents before we join the caravan."

Mary put her hand on her belly and smiled. "I know they are expecting us."

Joachim led his big donkey Henry toward Mary and Joseph when he saw them coming. Ann ran to her daughter with her arms wide open and tears in her eyes.

Mary's eyes shifted from her father, to her mother, then back to her father. "Please don't worry about us," Mary pleaded. "God is with us."

Joachim spoke and raised the reins toward his daughter. "Mary, I want you to ride Henry. This trip is too much for little Jeremiah."

Mary rubbed her donkey's neck. "No Papa, Jeremiah will take care of me."

Ann looked at Joseph with her eyebrows raised, and whispered, "She never says 'No' to her father."

"I think this time she knows what is best," Jospeh whispered back.

"Daughter," Joachim pleaded. "There are robbers and wild animals along these roads. You need a stronger animal to take care of you."

"My donkey was born for this." Mary spoke in a soft voice. "My Baby is the Son of God, no harm will come to us."

Ann put her arm around her husband's waist. "Our daughter is right. God will protect them."

Jospeh mounted Starlight while Joachim and Ann kissed their daughter good-bye.

Ann wiped tears from her eyes, as she and Joachim watched

Mary and Joseph disappear down the long dusty road with the caravan.

Starlight and Jeremiah took turns guarding Joseph and Mary throughout the night. As Joseph tucked his wife in her blankets, he noticed the two animals putting their heads together in a serious conversation.

"Starlight," Joseph chuckled. "What is Jeremiah saying to you?" The mule tossed his head in Joseph's direction, as if to say, "Mind your own business," then turned back to the donkey.

The donkey nodded. Mary chuckled, "My little donkey is giving instructions to your big mule."

"Instructions about what?" Joseph raised his eyebrows and laughed.

"Jeremiah is probably telling Starlight about the star we are following."

"I noticed that star," Joseph looked up and stared. "God is guiding us." He put his arm around Mary, kissed her forehead, then fell fast asleep.

Jeremiah stood guard for the first couple of hours, while Starlight slept. The howling of a pack of wild dogs could be heard in a distance. Jeremiah listened, as the howling grew closer. Minutes later, he could see many sets of eyes glowing in the dark night. The eyes stared at the sleeping caravan.

The donkey took a few steps toward the pack, stomped his little hoof and grunted. The wild pack stopped howling. One by one, the sets of glowing eyes turned and disappeared into the night. Jeremiah sighed with relief and kept watch until it was Starlight's turn.

The next night thee robbers approached the caravan

as Starlight was standing guard. The mule brayed and woke everyone in the caravan except for Joseph and Mary. Jeremiah and Starlight flattened their big ears back with their mouths open and walked toward the robbers.

"Thunderation!" One of the robbers screeched. The three robbers fled.

Jeremiah bent down and sniffed Mary and Joseph. When he was sure they were okay, he walked over to Starlight who had broken out in a sweat. The donkey nuzzled the big mule, then went back to sleep.

Each day, the trip became harder for Mary. As they made frequent stops for rest, the caravan got farther and farther ahead of them. By the time they reached the Jordan River, they were on their own.

"Let's stop here for the night," Joseph said. "I can fish in the river and there's plenty of plants for the animals to eat."

He helped Mary down, then tended to Jeremiah and Starlight. He built a little camp fire for Mary to warm herself, then went to the river to fish.

"It's a big one!" Joseph laughed as he pulled in his net. Mary stretched her neck from under the blankets as she watched her husband with delight. He cleaned the fish and cooked it on the fire. When they were finished eating, Joseph made a bed for Mary under a bush where she would be warm and safe.

The next morning, as they rode away from their camp, violent gusts of wind threw sand across their path.

"Ouch," Mary whispered and pulled her veil closer to her face.

"It's not going to be a pleasant traveling day." Joseph spoke sympathetically and moved Starlight closer to Mary, to protect her from the wind. As the hours passed, the clouds grew darker and the rain started. Joseph pointed to a cave, that wasn't too far ahead. "Hold on Mary," he tapped his heels against his mule. Both Starlight and Jeremiah hastened their pace until they reached the cave. The four of them huddled together to keep warm. When the rain stopped, they drank water from the Jordan, then continued on their journey.

The next day, Mary pulled her veil back, and looked up at the clear sky. She closed her eyes as the sunshine warmed her face. Joseph looked over and smiled at her. "Much nicer day today."

"Praise God for that," Mary opened her eyes and smiled back at him.

A few hours later, Jospeh stopped and studied his surroundings. "This must be the road that the caravan takes to go around Samaria,"

"Probably," Mary shrugged her shoulders. "But that will take us too far out of our way. I don't think there is time for that."

"Mary," Joseph cleared his throat. "The Samaritans have never been nice to us Jews. Surely they will make trouble for us."

"Joseph," Mary put her hand to her belly. "The star is not pointing to the road that goes around Samaria. It is pointing to the road that goes through Samaria. We need to take the shorter route. The Baby will arrive soon."

Joseph knew better than to argue with Mary, who was carrying the Son of God. He bowed his head and whispered, "We will follow the star."

Joseph held his breath and rode Starlight down the mountain

and into the village of Samaria, with Mary and Jeremiah close to his side.

It was market day in the village. Donkey and mule carts lined the streets; camels stood together at a hitching post. Vendors were busy selling products; purchasers were busy making bargains and packing their carts.

As they passed through the village, the donkeys, mules, and camels, acknowledge their presence and bowed their heads. However to the Samaritans, Joseph and Mary were invisible.

As they rode back up the mountain, Joseph let out a deep sigh, and put his hand on Mary's shoulder.

"Did you expect anything less?" She chuckled at her husband.

Joseph chuckled back at her. "Oh, Mary, you are so wise."

As night began to fall, they passed a cave opening where a mother lion sat, grooming her cubs. They were so tired they didn't even notice the lions until they were only a few feet away. The mother lion purred and pulled her cubs close to her. Jeremiah smacked his lips, and bowed his head in peace. The mother lion closed her eyes and bowed her head in response; her babies did the same.

A couple of nights later, as the sun began to set, the star led them along a path on the side of a mountain. Joseph gently pulled back the reins, and asked Starlight to stop. "There's Bethlehem!" He proudly pointed to the twinkling town lights below. "In less than an hour, you will be in a nice warm bed." Joseph smiled at Mary with relief. "Can you hold out that long?"

"I guess I'll have to," Mary tried to laugh, but her voice was shaky and Jospeh knew there was very little time.

"Mary hold on," he took a rein from her and tapped his heels against Starlight's side. "Come on Jeremiah, try to walk a little faster and keep up with Starlight."

As they entered the town of Bethlehem, Jeremiah tried to pull away from Starlight and walk toward a cave. Joseph, tugged on the rein, "No Jeremiah, we need to find an inn for Mary and the Baby."

"But the star is that way," Mary protested and pointed to the star above a stable inside a cave.

"I'll take the animals to the stable after I get you settled in a room." Joseph kept pushing the animals forward in search of an inn.

On the door of the first inn, a sign read 'No Rooms'. Joseph grumbled and hurried to the second inn. He saw people waiting in line at the door. He quickly jumped down from Starlight and tied him to the post. "Hold on Mary," he pleaded and handed her Jeremiah's rein. "I'll be back in a minute."

Joseph pushed his way through the line. He didn't want to be rude, but Mary needed a bed in a hurry. The baby was coming and time was running out.

As soon as Joseph was out of sight, Starlight untied the reins. He and Jeremiah turned and walked quickly to the stable that was under the star. Mary didn't protest, she trusted her donkey.

A little mule greeted Jeremiah at the door, then stepped back to let them enter. A big mule was lying in a pile of straw, keeping the spot warm for Mary. She stood up and Jeremiah gently laid down so Mary could slide off.

Starlight turned and raced back to the inn to get Joseph.

Meanwhile, the inn keeper showed Joseph mercy. "I am sorry, Sir, but I don't have any rooms, but you are welcome to stay in the stable. All of the animals have been put in for the night. You and your wife will have privacy there."

Joseph sighed with disappointment.

"Go quickly," the inn keeper advised. "There's no charge for you or your animals."

When Joseph came out of the inn, Starlight was waiting at the door. Joseph looked around in a panic. "Where's Mary?" Then he remembered Jeremiah veering to the cave under the star. It was the same cave the inn keeper offered. He quickly jumped up on Starlight's back and took off at a full gallop to the cave's entrance.

Starlight watched from the doorway, as all of the animals formed a circle around Mary and breathed on her to kept her warm.

Only the animals and Joseph saw the Baby Jesus make His entrance into the world. Mary wrapped Him in little blankets and placed Him in a manger.

Joseph picked up his head and noticed Starlight standing in the doorway with the cart still attached. "Oh my sweet mule," he hurried outside to tend to him.

Starlight sighed and nuzzled Joseph's head as he unhooked the shafts. Then something in the meadows caught his attention. He quickly picked up his head with his eyes wide and nostrils flaring. His big ears pointed in the direction of a light and beautiful music drifting across the meadow.

"What is it?" As Joseph studied the light, it began to form a shape. "Angels," Joseph whispered, "a multitude of angels dancing in the sky and blowing trumpets!"

The angels floated down and spoke to the shepherds who were tending their sheep.

"The angels are telling the shepherds about our Baby Jesus." Joseph gently rubbed the mule's head. They observed as the angels ascended back to the Heavens and the shepherds began walking in their direction.

Starlight blinked as he guarded the cave's entrance. For the next couple of hours, shepherds visited. They knelt next to the manger and gave praises to God.

When the last shepherd left, Starlight could hardly keep his eyes open. He watched Mary take the Baby out of the manger and hold Him in her arms as she laid down in the straw for the night. Joseph laid close at her side and Jeremiah laid close on her other side, both keeping her warm.

Another mule stood up from his place in the straw. He nodded to Starlight, then took Starlight's place guarding the door.

Starlight entered the cave and kissed Baby Jesus. He laid down in the straw and let out a deep sigh. Before closing his eyes, he looked one more time at the Holy Family sleeping safely and soundly. His mission was complete. He stretched out in the straw and fell fast asleep.

Lizzie's Lesson

*L*izzie's mother hung up the telephone, then put her hand across her mouth and looked away from Lizzie. "I know that was Mr. Flynn," Lizzie looked puzzled at her mother. "Doesn't he want me to try out for the Christmas pageant in Newark?"

"Well," her mother said in a calm voice. She sat down beside Lizzie and stroked her long dark hair. "The pastor of the church where the pageant will be held, picked the kids he wants to play in the pageant."

"You mean, someone else is playing Mary?"

Her mother nodded, "I am sorry, Sweetie. Someone else has been picked for the part."

"That is not fair!" Lizzie jumped up from the couch. "Mr. Flynn told me he wanted me to audition!"

"Oh Lizzie, I'm sorry. Mr. Flynn did want you to audition, but someone else picked the cast and Mr. Flynn had nothing to do with it."

Lizzie stood in the middle of the living room, clenching her fists as tears rolled down her cheeks. "But he promised!"

"I understand," her mother smiled. "You will still be a part of our church's pageant and there will be other pageants."

Lizzie took a deep breath and wiped the tears away. "I know Mama. I am going to call Flip and give her the news. She won't be so upset because she is playing Mary at our church this year."

As Lizzie marched to her room, her mother called after her. "And you played Mary last year."

For the next couple weeks Lizzie and Flip rode Hannah's donkeys, Christopher and Crystal, every day after school. Daylight was getting shorter as the winter season was approaching.

"I think the pageant in Newark is this weekend," Flip said to her cousin as they rode the donkeys back to the barn.

"Probably," Lizzie looked the other way.

"Don't you want to go and see it? Don't you remember Mr. Flynn asked Hannah if he could use the donkeys?"

"I am not interested." Lizzie answered as she ran her fingers through Christopher's thick coat.

"Stop being a bad sport!" Flip scolded.

"I am not being a bad sport!" Lizzie shouted and caught Hannah's attention.

"What's this I hear?" Hannah pushed a lock of gray hair under her wool cap as she approached the girls.

"Oh nothing," Lizzie mumbled and looked away from Hannah.

"I know you are upset because you didn't get the part in the pageant, but there will be other pageants and other parts." Hannah spoke nonchalantly as she gave a little candy cane to each of her donkeys.

"I know," Lizzie huffed then led Christopher into the barn.

Flip waited until Lizzie was out of earshot, then whispered to Hannah, "She's not taking this very well."

Hannah looked in Lizzie's direction and shook her head. "She'll have to get over it."

Saturday morning Hannah and Flip groomed the donkeys and shared donkey stories while Lizzie sat by herself and polished the brass buckles on the halters. Hannah's husband, Troy, entered the barn rubbing his hands together and chuckling. "The trailer is ready and the cold weather has arrived!"

"Do you think they need blankets for the ride?" Hannah questioned her husband.

"The doors in the trailer will be closed and they have enough hair to keep them warm." He looked at Lizzie who was keeping her head down as she folded the rags and put the lid back on the polish can. "The halters look good," he said cheerfully as he held them up to admire. "Come on Lizzie, we have to load the donkeys on the trailer now."

It was a two hour ride from Hannah and Troy's barn to the church in Newark, New Jersey. Lizzie sat in silence staring out the window. Flip was very entertained as she listened to Hannah and Troy tell snow storm stories. "I've never seen a six foot snow drift!" She exclaimed.

"Well you might if you stay in New Jersey!" Hannah smiled back at her.

"Welcome to the city of Newark," Troy mumbled as he drove into the church parking lot, looking for a place to park.

"It looks like a lot of people live here," Flip took off her seat belt and leaned forward in between Troy and Hannah. "This church is gigantic! Look at the tall steeple!"

A police officer wearing an orange vest approached them and pointed to a parking spot near the door of an auditorium.

"Why are the police here?" Lizzie whispered as she took off her seat belt and peered out the window.

"In cities like this, there are usually a lot of police because there are a lot of people," Troy spoke in a matter of fact tone as he parked the truck.

"I assume you have the donkeys," the policeman smiled as Troy got out of the truck.

Troy held out his hand and chuckled. "I am Troy, and I have the donkeys."

The policeman shook Troy's hand. "You can take them through that door and into a courtyard." Then looking at the trailer, he whispered, "Did you bring provisions to clean up after them?"

Troy laughed, "I don't leave home without provisions to clean up!"

The policeman's face turned red and he looked away. "Sorry, but I needed to make sure. Let me know if you need anything. I'll be in the parking lot."

The donkeys brayed softly as Troy lowered the trailer ramp. Lizzie opened the front door and took out the manure bucket, broom and shovel.

"I'll clean up." Troy said as he handed the donkeys to the girls and motioned to Hannah. "I'll meet you in the courtyard after I clean the trailer and lock up."

Inside the courtyard was a world all of its own. Brown grass covered the ground and the stone walls were lined with bushes and park benches. Hannah looked around and was happy to see a water faucet with a hose. The donkeys looked around for a few seconds then put their heads down and munched on the grass.

"Stay here, while I get a water bucket," Hannah instructed and closed the courtyard door behind her.

As Hannah and Troy were entering the courtyard, Mr. Flynn opened the back door of the auditorium and greeted them. His eyes fell on Lizzie, "I am so glad to see you. I need you to talk to Dahlia, the girl who is playing Mary."

Lizzie looked up at Hannah with her mouth opened. No words came out, but the expression in her eyes pleaded that she didn't want to meet the girl who was playing Mary. Hannah raised her eyebrows and nodded her head toward Mr. Flynn.

"Ahh ..of course," Lizzie forced a smile and walked toward Mr. Flynn.

He sighed in relief, then put his hand on Lizzie's shoulder and whispered.

"Dahlia was picked for the part because she can't walk."

"What?" Lizzie's face crinkled.

"As you know, Mary sits on the donkey for most of her part. When she sings the closing song, Joseph will be standing next to her for support."

"So what is the problem?" Lizzie raised her hands with her palms up.

"Suddenly she's afraid of donkeys," Mr. Flynn shook his head. They walked down a hall and stopped in front of a door. Before opening the door he whispered to Lizzie. "I know you can help her."

"Dahlia," Mr. Flynn spoke softly to a little girl in a wheelchair with a book on her lap. "This is Lizzie. She rides Christopher, the donkey you will be riding in the pageant."

"I don't like donkeys," Dahlia spoke with her eyes closed, clenching the book with both hands.

Mr. Flynn gently patted Lizzie's shoulder then left the room.

Lizzie stared at Dahlia who was not looking back at her. She was about Lizzie's age, but couldn't do the things that Lizzie took for granted.

Lizzie put her head down and squeezed her eyes shut. She felt her face redden with shame. How could she feel so hostile toward this little girl? She walked close to Dahlia and spoke. "Can I see what you are reading?"

Dahlia let go of the book as Lizzie gently took it from her and opened it. "This is a nice book," Lizzie turned the pages. "If you read it, you will learn how donkeys are great protectors." Then she turned to a photo of a donkey holding a fox by the back of its neck. "Look at this!" Lizzie held the book up for Dahlia to see.

"The donkey killed the fox!" Dahlia broke into tears.

"It didn't kill the fox," Lizzie tone was firm. "The donkey lifted the fox and threw it away from her baby." Lizzie read the page to Dahlia. "She was protecting her baby. Wouldn't your Mama do the same for you?"

The girls' eyes met, then they broke into laughter.

"I don't know that my Mama would grab a fox by the back of the neck." Dahlia wiped the tears from her cheeks.

"Well you know what I mean," Lizzie giggled, then moved her chair closer to Dahlia. "I'll tell you everything I know about Christopher. He is the best donkey in the world! His stable mate, Crystal, is also here and she is the second best donkey in the world."

Dahlia's eyes grew wide as Lizzie told her stories about her donkey adventures with her cousin, Flip.

"Where's your coat?" Lizzie asked her. "I'll push you out to the courtyard so you can meet the donkeys and my cousin Flip."

As the girls chatted, Ray, the sheep owner brought three sheep onto the stage and locked them in the stall that was part of the Nativity scene. "It looks sturdy enough," Ray commented to Mr. Flynn as he pushed against the gate. "As long as they have hay, they will be content. I'm going to get a cup of coffee. I'll be right back."

As Lizzie pushed the wheelchair through the back door, Flip was approaching. "The camel is here! Where's Mr. Flynn?"

Lizzie looked back and saw Mr. Flynn walking in her direction. "The camel is here," she shouted, then turned back to Flip. "This is Dahlia, she is playing the Blessed Mother in the pageant and she needs to meet the donkeys."

As Lizzie spoke, the camel was being led through the courtyard door.

"Who is going to ride the camel?" Dahlia giggled.

"I don't know anything about that," her voice trailed off as she clenched the wheel chair handles. She could see Troy and Hannah speaking to a young man who held the camel. Something in her stomach didn't feel right. She pushed the wheelchair to a bench where Flip was sitting, keeping the donkeys company.

"I don't know about this," Flip whispered to her.

"Me neither," Lizzie responded.

"I heard the man tell Troy, the camel is only a year old." Hannah looked up at the camel but she wasn't smiling. The camel moved from side to side as his handler kept his focus on Troy and didn't seem to be bothered by the camel's unruliness.

"It's good to see you," Mr. Flynn greeted the handler and walked very quickly toward the camel. He was only a few feet away, when the camel spit at Mr. Flynn.

"Oh!" Mr. Flynn yelled, then stared at the camel's saliva

on his brown suede jacket. He crinkled his nose, pulled out a handkerchief and quickly wiped his jacket. He huffed, then raised his chin and beckoned to the man holding the camel. "I'll show you to the stage."

"Come on," the young man spoke to the camel as he followed Mr. Flynn. They had only taken a few steps when the camel noticed the donkeys on the other side of the courtyard. The camel grunted then began to pull his handler toward the donkeys.

Christopher and Crystal huddled close to the girls and turned their hind ends toward the camel and kicked out.

The camel spit toward the donkeys, then turned his head back to his handler.

Christopher's head was in Dahlia's lap as the camel exited the courtyard. His big ears wiggled back and forth brushing the hair away from her face.

She giggled. "I see what you mean about donkeys being protective."

"He likes you," Lizzie stroked Christopher's ear. "Take you hand and gently rub the inside of his ear like this."

At first Dahlia was hesitant, then she let her fingers gently slide up and down the donkey's long soft ear. Christopher closed his eyes and brayed softly. Dahlia started giggling and Christopher brayed a little louder.

"Can I hug him?" Dahlia asked.

"Of course you can," Lizzie answered.

"You better hug Crystal too," Flip teased. "She will get jealous."

Lizzie turned in her seat and observed Dahlia interacting with the donkeys and giggling with Flip. She smiled sweetly and a lump formed in her throat. "She deserves to play Mary in the pageant," she whispered. "I have taken so much for granted."

"This stall is for the camel," Mr. Flynn pointed to a small wooden structure that was to hold the big animal.

The handler laughed but led the camel into the stall anyway. "I don't think this is going to work," he said looking at the wooden structure that was almost as tall as the camel's legs.

No sooner did he get the words out of his mouth, the camel let out a loud startling grunt and pulled away from the handler. Stepping over the stall gate, he headed for the sheep.

Stall boards flew across the stage as the panicked sheep broke out and ran through the auditorium. The young camel playfully jumped and grunted as he chased the sheep. The handler stood on the stage with his mouth open, not knowing what to do.

"This doesn't sound good," Troy spoke to Hannah as they came in from the courtyard. He ran ahead of her, then stopped at the entrance of the auditorium.

"Get that camel out of here!" Mr. Flynn demanded.

"What's going on?" Ray stood in the back doorway holding a cup of coffee. The sheep heard his voice and raced toward him, while the camel continued to hop and grunt. He quickly opened the door, let the sheep slip through, then closed the door behind them.

"Know anything about camels?" Troy raised his eye brows trying to ease the tension.

"I brought some apples and carrots," a little boy entered from the back stage.

"Excellent," the handler sighed. He took one of the apples and approached the camel with his hand extended. The camel walked toward his handler with his nose out expecting the treat.

"I'll herd the sheep back stage while you go through with the camel," Ray said.

"I'll follow the camel," Troy nodded to Ray. Then yelled to Hannah, "Get a hold of the donkeys."

As the camel was led through the courtyard, the little boy walked close to the handler keeping him occupied with carrots and apples.

The camel continued his pace and walked obediently on the truck. Troy closed the door behind him. The handler stepped out the side door of the truck, apologized, then drove off.

Troy put his hand on the little boy's shoulder as they walked back to the courtyard. "You saved the day, Little Man."

"My name is Travis," the boy answered. "I'm playing Joseph in the pageant."

"That's my big brother!" Dahlia chimed in.

Mr. Flynn looked at his watch. "We have forty-five minutes to get everything cleaned up before dress rehearsal begins."

"Are there anymore animals coming?" Troy asked as he picked up the broken wood from the sheep stall.

"No more animals!" Mr. Flynn replied in hast.

"Travis," Troy beckoned. "Help me dismantle this stall and throw it into the dumpster. The sheep will go in the other stall that was built for the camel."

"Sure!" Travis answered and hurried to the stage.

Troy, Travis, and Ray put the stage back together while Hannah, Lizzie, and Flip cleaned up camel and sheep manure.

"This is fun," Dahlia giggled as she and Mr. Flynn wiped camel hairs from the auditorium chairs.

"So how many are in the cast?" Hannah asked as she finished cleaning.

"We have twelve kids in this production." Mr. Flynn put the bucket on Dahlia's lap and pushed her wheelchair toward the stage. "The Leer sisters make up five of the cast members, ranging in age from eight to fifteen." He stopped and brushed his forehead with his sleeve. "They belong to a choir in New York City that keeps them pretty busy. I only had the girls for two nights to teach them the songs. We practiced and practiced and practiced."

"I think you practiced a little too hard," a woman's voice spoke from the doorway.

Mr. Flynn turned and faced five little girls standing with their mother. Their faces were red and the two youngest were holding their hands over their throats.

"What's going on?" He asked in horror.

"They lost their voices from too much practice!" The woman answered sharply.

The oldest girl stepped forward and whispered. "I can't sing, but I can still dance." The other four girls nodded their heads in unison.

"Oh no!" Mr. Flynn put both of his hands to his head.

Lizzie and Flip both looked at each other and hurried toward him. Lizzie bellowed, "Mr. Flynn, Flip and I know all of the songs."

Mr. Flynn let go of his head and chuckled, "Thank God for you girls. The stage manager will find costumes for both of you."

The dress rehearsal went on as scheduled. Lizzie helped Dahlia with Christopher and Flip helped Travis with Crystal. The Leer sisters danced, the shepherds and inn keepers said their lines. Lizzie and Flip's angelic voices filled the auditorium. In the closing scene, Dahlia stood close to her brother and sang "Oh

Holy Night." Her voice was soft and sweet, but could hardly be heard.

"I'm shy when I sing." Dahlia's cheeks grew red and she put her head down.

"I've got you covered," Lizzie pushed the wheelchair up to her and motioned for her to sit. "We are going back stage and having a singing lesson." She looked at Flip and beckoned. Flip followed her to the backstage.

"Sing from here," Flip put her hand to her stomach.

Dahlia's eyes sparkled as she responded to everything the girls told her to do.

"Open your mouth and sing louder," Lizzie instructed.

As Dahlia sang, the notes became clear and 'Oh Holy Night' came to life.

Dahlia and Travis's parents were the first to arrive in the auditorium. They sat in the front row. Their father nervously tapped his foot on the floor as he waited impatiently. Their mother put her hand on his knee and whispered. "Relax, they will do just fine."

"I'm sure they will," he huffed and kept his feet still, then started tapping his thumb on his knee. She looked at him and chuckled.

At 7:00, the auditorium lights blinked. When everyone was seated, the house lights were turned off and the music began. A spotlight fell on the two donkeys as they made their way to the stage. The first inn keeper delivered the opening line and the play began to unfold.

Lizzie and Flip watched as the donkeys moved from station to station with Travis and Dahlia on their backs. Dahlia's face glowed. "She looks so natural on the donkey," Lizzie whispered to Flip.

"Thanks to you," Flip whispered back.

The Leer sisters took the stage and danced, keeping the audience on the edge of their seats.

When Lizzie and Flip sang, Mr. Flynn smiled in relief, then sat back in his chair.

Dahlia stood center stage with a Baby Jesus doll in her arms. Her brother stood close behind her, with his hands on her shoulders. The music began and she sang the first line of "Oh Holy Night." With each note, her voice grew with confidence. When she reached the final verse, her angelic voice could be heard for blocks around. Her mother wiped the tears from her eyes and all was silent in the auditorium.

The silence was broken when Christopher and Crystal decided they had enough show time, and let out a loud bray. First the audience chuckled, then everyone stood up and cheered. Dahlia turned to Lizzie and threw her a kiss. Lizzie threw a kiss back to her as tears rolled down her cheeks.

She taught Dahlia about donkeys and she taught her how to sing. But more importantly was the lesson that she learned from Dahlia.

"Praise you Jesus," Lizzie whispered, "and Happy Birthday,"

Papeta's Performance

November winds howled outside the church hall where the 4H annual banquet was taking place.

Angelina sat at a little table with her parents, Carlos and Rayna. She was extremely self-conscious and cold. She grew up in Mexico and arrived in New Jersey during the spring, when the weather was nice. November winds was something she had never experienced. There was so much in this town that she had never experienced. At home she had lots of friends and everyone was equal. In her new town in central NJ, that was not the case. In September she started her freshman year in a big high school. She only knew a few of the girls she met over the summer through 4H. They were not very nice to her.

She sat with her head down, staring at her placemat wondering why she even joined 4H in the first place.

Earlier that year, her father, Carlos, landed an excellent job on a Thoroughbred breeding farm. When his boss, Mr. Harris learned he had a wife and daughter still living in Mexico he sent for them and the daughter's pet mule as well.

"I never had a mule on the property," he chuckled to Carlos while patting him on the shoulder. "My daughter Diana will introduce your daughter to the other kids in the area who have horses. She will look out for your little girl."

Diana was very sure of herself and did look out for Angelina. She was a beautiful girl with long blonde hair and big blue eyes. She was a senior at the same high school, but unfortunately, their paths rarely crossed during the school day.

Diana no longer spent time with the horses or the 4H club. She was an avid dancer and an honor roll student. When she was not at the studio dancing, she was in her room studying. She had hopes of attending law school. Diana thought she was doing Angelina a favor by enrolling her in the Regal Riders 4H Club with four girls she would be going to school with. The only problem was the girls were unaccepting of Angelina because she was different.

Besides having fancy show horses, Shelia, Mary Beth, Teresa and Barbra sported the latest designer fashions and kept themselves thin and fit. Appearance was most important to them.

Angelina had a pet mule that she rode bareback because she never owned a saddle. She knew nothing about horse shows. She was short and plump and wore the same clothes she wore in Mexico.

Mrs. Benson stepped up to the microphone and the room grew quiet. She was an older woman and involved with 4H for many years. She knew all of the kids' names and the names of their horses. She began with the pleasures by thanking everyone for attending and acknowledging all of the different 4H horse clubs. Then she turned and picked up a trophy from the awards table. It was a wooden trophy with a bronze color horse on top.

"It is my pleasure to present this award to Daniela Wilson for Western Horsemanship."

Everyone clapped while Daniela walked up to the front of the banquet hall to receive her award.

The award ceremony continued for an hour while each recipient captured the attention of everyone in the room.

Angelina began to feel self-conscious about walking to the front of the hall with everyone watching her. She was told that every child would receive an award. She knew since she had only been a member for a short time, she had't done anything to deserve an award.

Angelina's mother looked at her and questioned, "When is it your turn?"

Angelina thought to herself, "Never, I hope," but instead she smiled at her mom and said, "I don't know."

Angelina's father leaned over and grinned at the two of them as if he knew something.

"Our last award is a special award," Mrs. Benson proudly announced and the room grew silent as she held up the last trophy from the awards table. To everyone's surprise, the trophy was a bronze mule instead of a bronze horse.

"Ooooo's" and "Ahhhh'a" could be heard around the room.

Her father, Carlos, sat up and raised his chest. Her mother, Rayna, looked around, then put her head down and covered her mouth to hide her excitement.

Mrs. Benson continued, "I am calling this award, 'The Uniqueness Award'!"

Angelina closed her eyes, and felt the heat rise to her face as her cheeks grow bright red. She wished the floor would open up and swallow her inside.

"Angelina Lopez, please come up here and receive this award."

Angelina opened her eyes and quickly made her way to the front of the hall. "Get this over with as quickly as possible she thought to herself." On her way, she could hear the mean whispers of her four classmates, "Hee haw, Hee haw, she's the ugliest ass I ever saw."

Pain stabbed at her heart with the thought that her parents would hear this mocking.

Mrs. Benson introduced Angelina as the 4H Newcomer. She told everyone how Mr. Harris brought her family and her molly mule from Mexico to New Jersey. Mrs. Benson continued her speech telling everyone how happy she was to have Angelina and Papeta, her molly mule, in the 4H community.

The audience clapped and Angelina felt a wave of relief. A photographer took a picture as Mrs. Benson handed her the trophy.

As she walked back to her table, her eyes focused on her parents' radiant smiles. She was not watching where she was walking and came very close to the table where her classmates sat. She could hear one of them say, "I can't believe she wore that ugly dress to the banquet." Then another girl said, "I wish she and that stupid mule of hers would go back to Mexico. They are an embarrassment to our club."

Angelina wanted to cry, but as she looked at her proud father, she did not want to ruin the moment for him.

Her father's eyes lit up as she approached him, but her mother's eyes told a different story. Angelina guessed her mother heard what she heard and it hurt.

The next morning Angelina stood in the stall with Papeta, her arms wrapped around her molly's neck. "I don't know why those girls are so mean to us. You are the most beautiful molly in the whole world. They don't know what they are talking about."

Papeta lowered her head and pressed it against Angelina

chest. Papeta knew how to comfort her girl. Angelina scratched her molly's ears and continued to sob. "Maybe we should go back to Mexico; no one likes us here."

Just then Diana burst through the barn door. "What's going on in here? You can't just get up and leave us!"

Angelina idolized Diana and she cried harder as Diana approached.

"Oh Little Angel," as Diana so affectionately nick named her. "Why are you crying?"

Angelina proceeded to tell Diana about the four girls who were so mean to her. "They even said the dress I was wearing was ugly. It is my best dress, how can it be ugly?"

As Angelina cried, Diana put her arms around her and stroked her long black hair. Then she changed her tone, stepped back and placed her hands on Angelina's shoulders. "We'll go clothes shopping tonight, but right now we need you at the church."

Diana stared mischievously into Angelina's eyes.

"Why do you need me?" She giggled drying her eyes.

"Sherry broke her ankle last night at the basketball game," Diana continued staring at Angelina. Sherry was Diana's best friend and also looked after Angelina.

"What?" Angelina's voice grew loud and her eyes grew wide.

"She was making a jump shot and landed wrong. She will be okay in six weeks but now she can't be in the Christmas pageant that is to take place in four weeks."

"Oh no!" Angelina sighed. "She was so excited to be playing the Blessed Mother. What will happen now?"

Diana put her hand on Angelina's face, took a deep breath

and smiled. "I told Mrs. Carrelli that you would play the Blessed Mother."

"Me?" Angelina pointed to herself.

"Yes, you," Diana said grinning from ear to ear. "You have a beautiful voice Little Angel. I often stand outside the barn door and listen to you sing to Papeta. Today I came here and I heard you crying."

For a moment Angelina put her head down and pictured herself dressed as the Blessed Mother standing in front of an audience. "Playing the Blessed Mother is such an honor," she said as she picked her head up and looked at Diana for reassurance.

"Come on, we need to go. Brush the hay off of your coat, clean the manure off of your shoes and get in the car." Diana had a way of ordering her little friend in a comic fashion.

As Angelina was fastening her seat belt, Diana pressed her lips together, then spoke in a quiet tone. "I told Mrs. Carrelli you would ride Papeta down the aisle and across the stage in the performance."

"Diana!" Angelina looked horrified. "The Blessed Mother rode a donkey not a mule!"

Diana raised her chin and answered back, "The bible does not tell us how Mary and Joseph traveled to Bethlehem. How do we know it was not a mule instead of a donkey?"

The two girls looked at each other and Diana's tone grew serious. "All we really do know is that they did not take a bus."

They laughed hard then Angelina shook her head and continued, "In all of the pictures, the Blessed Mother was riding a donkey."

Diana stopped the car at the end of the driveway. With a witty smile she leaned toward her young friend, "You are a Mexican girl playing the part of a Jewish girl. So why can't Papeta, a mule, play the part of a donkey?"

Both girls burst into laughter again.

"It's settled," Diana said with a grin. "I told Mrs. Carrelli she could count on both of you!"

Diana drove into the church parking lot in her red Mercedes Benz Sport's Car. Angelina always felt secure around Diana, but riding shot gun with her in that car was something extra special.

"We will practice here for the next five weeks and then we move to the high school auditorium for final dress rehearsals and the show. Papeta will come to one or two dress rehearsals until she is comfortable."

Angelina looked up at Diana with a radiant smile. "This is going to be so much fun."

As the girls walked across the parking lot, Diana waved to a couple of her friends. They waved back and acknowledged Angelina.

Diana's boyfriend Dominic, called to Angelina in Spanish. "Little Angel, I am so glad you are here to help us."

"Is Dominic going to be in the show?" Angelina looked up at Diana with her mouth open and her big brown eyes even bigger.

"Dominic plays St. Joseph." She raised her eyebrows then put her arm around her little friend. "And your neighbor, Lenny, is playing the inn keeper.

Mrs. Carrelli noticed Diana and Angelina walking through the doorway. She stopped what she was doing and approached Angelina with her arms extended. "Little Angel, I have heard so much about you. Welcome aboard!"

As Mrs. Carrelli moved toward her, Angelina's eyes shifted

around the room. All eyes were on her to welcome her. Her face lit up and she felt butterflies in her stomach. She giggled softly, as she was lost for words.

Mrs. Carrelli took her by the hand and whispered warmly. "I head you have the most beautiful voice. I'm glad to finally meet you."

Angelina put her head down and whispered, "Thank you."

Then Mrs. Carrelli put her arm around Angelina's shoulder and spoke aloud to everyone in the room. "Everyone, I want you to come and meet our new cast member."

Twenty five cast and crew members stopped what they were doing and formed a circle around Angelina, Mrs. Carrelli and Diana. Mrs. Carrelli motioned to Diana to do the introduction.

Diana glanced down at Little Angel and smiled before speaking. "Everyone, I want to introduce my very special friend Angelina Lopez. She is going to play the Blessed Mother in our pageant."

Everyone clapped and shouted warm welcomes. Angelina put her head down and raised her shoulders toward her face almost trying to hide. Mrs. Carrelli sensed the girl's embarrassment. Drawing her closer she whispered, "Are you ready for your first practice?"

Angelina shook her head 'yes' as Mrs. Carrelli released her hug. Another girl she recognized from school stepped in front of her. "I don't think we ever met. I am Joanie, the stage manager. This is your script." She handed Angelina a booklet.

She took the booklet from Joanie and looked up at Diana and Mrs. Carrelli with question in her eyes.

Mrs. Carrelli quickly explained. "This is the story that we

are about to perform." She opened the booklet and explained to Angelina how to follow the script and do her part.

Angelina was in the first scene. The scene would take place in Mary's bedroom where the angel Gabriel appeared to her. Joanie walked through each scene with Angelina and explained where she would stand and when she would speak. Angelina caught on quickly. She was excited to take part in an activity where the other kids accepted her.

Mr. Harris and Carlos trailered Papeta to the first dress rehearsal at the high school auditorium. The entire cast and crew came out to the parking lot to meet her. Flattered to the point of embarrassment, Angelina stood in the parking lot holding her stocky little molly with four white socks and a white blaze. Papeta held her head high as she knew she was being showcased. Angelina shifted her eyes from her dad and Mr. Harris to the molly and the other kids. She couldn't help but giggle. Then Papeta let out a loud bray that caused some of the kids to jump back.

"What was that?" Someone laughed.

"That is called a 'bray'. A mule's bray is different from a donkey's bray."

"I know this mule's bray," Lenny chuckled, then walked with Angelina as she led Papeta into the auditorium. Angelina turned to Lenny with concern but still giggling, "I hope she does't do that during the show."

Lenny responded, "I hope she does't poop during the show."

Angelina's expression turned serious. "I won't feed her before we come."

"Good idea," Lenny said shaking his head.

Papeta's first scene was to walk down the aisle to the town

of Bethlehem. Angelina sat sideway on the molly while Dominic walked along side. When Papeta saw the bright lights on stage she started she brayed softly.

"Quick, put your hand over her nose," Angelina told him. Then she whispered to her molly, "Shhh Papeta, Shhhh."

"I think she understands," Dominic reassured her as the molly relaxed.

Papeta practiced walking down the aisle and walking across the stage several times during the first practice. Angelina and Mrs. Carrelli were certain she was ready for opening night.

The big night finally arrived, the Sunday before Christmas. Carlos and Rayna were more nervous than Angelina.

Rayna stood in the doorway of her daughter's bedroom. With tears in her eyes, she watched her daughter brush her long black hair. "Remember, you are singing for God."

"Yes, Momma I know," she smiled up at her mom. "The Blessed Mother is with me and I will play my part well."

Carlos came through the back door and announced, "Papeta is on the trailer and it is time to go."

Rayna kissed her daughter on the forehead and they walked out to the truck.

The backstage hustle and bustle gave Angelina butterflies in her stomach. Diana's friend Eleanor helped her put on her stage make up. Angelina had the giggles and couldn't keep a straight face.

"You have got to hold still," Eleanor ordered trying not to laugh with her.

"I have never worn so much make up," Angelina tried to

explain. "In Mexico, I would not be considered a nice girl if I went to school like this."

Eleanor grabbed Angelina's shoulder and gently shook it. "This is stage make up so the people in the back of the auditorium can see what you look like. Now hold still; it is getting close to curtain time."

Angelina only giggled all the more. Then Mrs. Carrelli peaked into the dressing room. "Angelina, you have fifteen minutes."

Angelina then grabbed Eleanor's hand and her giggles turned serious. "It is almost time!"

The lights dimmed in the auditorium and all grew quiet. Mrs. Carrelli walked Angelina to the stage wing and motioned for her to take her place on a bench in center stage. Angelina looked into the audience and her heart felt like it would jump out of her chest. Looking back into the stage wing, she saw several cast members smiling and giving her the thumbs up. "Go Angelina!" she heard Lenny whisper.

Then the spot light shone on the Blessed Mother and the play began. Angelina sat on the bench sewing a garment while singing the psalms. Then along side of her, another spot light shone and the Angel Gabriel appeared.

"Do not be afraid," he said to her and the scene continued.

When the scene finished, the lights went out, the two left the stage and the stage crew picked up the bench from center stage. Dominic was waiting for her in the wing. Taking her hand, he beckoned to her, "We have to hurry and get Papeta."

Angelina sat sideways on Papeta in the hallway in front of the doors to the auditorium while Dominic held the molly's halter and rubbed her long ears. Papeta looked as though she could fall asleep. Then the music began and the two of them peered through the window as the first dance scene began.

"Oh look at Diana. Isn't she beautiful?" Angelina whispered.

"That's my girl," Dominic smiled.

As the dancers made their way off the stage, Joanie opened the auditorium door and beckoned to them. Papeta's eyes opened and she pointed her big ears forward. Angelina could feel her back rise and an unwanted bray about to happen.

"Dominic, hold your hand over her nose," Angelina nervously instructed Dominic. "Shhhh, Papeta Shhh," she pleaded with the molly.

"I have her," Dominic reassured her as the three made their way down the auditorium aisle through the audience.

Someone whispered, "Mary is riding a live donkey!" Then throughout the audience 'uuuuuss' and 'awwwwwws' could be heard.

Dominic led the mule up the ramp and onto the stage. As he stopped at the first inn, Papeta glared into the audience and raised her back with her nostrils flaring. Angelina held her breathe and rubbed the molly's neck. Without missing a beat, as Dominic was delivering his lines, he rubbed the molly's nose. Papeta relaxed her back and closed her eyes.

Angelina could see her mother sitting in the first row and heard her whisper, "Buena mi burra."

The scene continued and Lenny appeared as the inn keeper who offered them a place in his stable. Next the three of them walked off stage and Carlos met them in the wing and took charge of Papeta. Angelina gave her dad a big hug and whispered, "Papeta is being a good girl."

He looked down at his daughter with tears in his eyes, "You are so beautiful tonight."

Choirs of angels filled the stage with dance and song. Diana leaped through the air and into the arms of her dance partner. He swung her around while Dominic held his breath. Angelina looked up at him and smiled, "I am so proud of her."

Dominic put his arm around her and gave her a big squeeze without saying a word and without taking his eyes off of Diana.

The music grew softer as the angels danced off the stage and the shepherds appeared front and center stage. The curtain closed behind them and cast and crew prepared for the next scene.

Carlos took Papeta to her spot on stage and stayed with her hiding himself behind the stable. Joanie handed Angelina a baby doll to portray the Baby Jesus and everyone took their spot on stage.

The bright star shone with almost blinding brightness while the curtain opened. The Baby Jesus was born. Shepherds gathered around the manger praising God while Papeta stood in the background. Angelina could hear Papeta chewing and she knew her dad was feeding her cookies to keep her quiet. She smiled to herself.

The stable grew dark and the spot light fell on Angelina. She stepped forward and began to sing "Silent Night." Her voice was more beautiful than anyone who ever performed on that high school stage. The audience was memorized as Angelina held the high notes with ease. Carlos was wiping the tears from his eyes when Papeta walked away from him and headed toward Angelina.

Only the lighting crew knew what she had planned. She

knew that one day she would show everyone that her molly was something very special. And that one day had finally arrived.

As Angelina continued her song, Papeta entered the spot light and knelt down along side of her as if in prayer. "Ahhhhs" were heard from the audience and Angelina continued singing. As she sang, she kept an eye on her molly and her molly knew she must behave.

As Angelina sang the last line, "Jesus Lord, at Thy birth," her voice softened and she bowed her head in prayer thanking God for a successful opening night. The song ended and all was quiet in the auditorium. Just as the curtain was about to close and the audience began to applause, Papeta could no longer contain herself and let out the loudest mule bray.

The audience stood up and clapped louder in spite of it.

Merry Christmas to all and Remember Jesus is the Reason for the Season!

Sir William's Delivery

The congregation broke into song, as Father Harold finished the final blessing at the Christmas Eve mass. Margaret's voice cracked when she sang, "Jesus Lord, at Thy birth." She turned her head and smiled at her three sons.

The boys were young adults now, but at times like Christmas, she wished they were kids again. She took a hold of her husband, George's hand.

"We have to go back to the shop to get something." Anthony informed his father when the song finished.

Anthony operated his own tractor repair business. His shop was five miles from their home.

"It's Christmas Eve!" George protested. "Your mother prepared a nice dinner for us."

George looked at Margaret for approval, but she was on her way to the Nativity Scene at the other end of the church.

"Well don't be long," George commanded as the boys rushed to the parking lot.

George stood behind Margaret while she knelt and prayed in front of the manger. He fidgeted with the zipper on his jacket for a few seconds before noticing the hay in the Nativity.

"It looks like the hay came from our barn?" He announced.

Margaret chuckled as she stood up and faced him. "Yes, the hay came from our barn. Sir William said it was okay to share some of his hay with the Baby Jesus."

"The boys drove back to the shop to get something," George informed her. "I told them to hurry."

"They will," Margaret responded in a quick tone, then hugged some of her friends and wished them a Merry Christmas.

"It is going to be a white Christmas," Glenda giggled and pointed out the window. The parking lot lights illuminated snowflakes gently falling from the night sky.

George held Margaret's arm as they walked to their car across the snow covered black top. A soft cold breeze blew across their faces and George broke into song, "I'm dreaming of a white Christmas."

Margaret finished the verse while holding up her hand to catch a snowflake, "Just like the ones I used to know." The two laughed as George opened the car door for her.

"I guess the boys will be plowing tonight," George sighed.

"Just Anthony and Jim, Baron will be with the firehouse delivering toys to the new shelter." Margaret's eyes gleamed as she recalled the toys she wrapped contributing to the cause. "I wish I could take them to the shelter myself."

"Maybe next year," George said in haste, as he assessed the snow covered roads.

"Let's take a drive through Mountain High Point and see all the beautiful Christmas lights!"

"What about dinner?" George looked back at her in disbelief.

"It will only take a few minutes," Margaret insisted. "Let's just enjoy the moment while the boys are gone."

George looked at her and raised his eyebrows. "She's up to

something," he thought to himself, then cleared his throat. "If you insist."

As they drove two miles through the housing development, Margaret studied each house. "Those are the most beautiful angels I have ever seen!"

"Very nice," George quickly responded, as they came to the end of the development. "Okay, that's enough. I hope the boys are back. I'm hungry."

Margaret giggled, "Yeah, me too!"

When they reached their driveway, the headlights of another vehicle was approaching.

"It's Anthony," George squinted and leaned closer to the window. "He's hauling something on his flatbed." He sat back and scratched his head. "Maybe he's delivering a tractor to someone for Christmas."

"Not quite!" Margaret giggled and put her hand on his shoulder. "Wait; let them pull in first."

"What's on the back of the flatbed?" George's face grew red as he began to share in his wife's excitement. "That's not a tractor!"

Anthony beeped the truck horn a couple of times while he and his brothers waved out the truck windows. "Merry Christmas Pops!"

As the truck and trailer turned into the driveway, a beautiful red sleigh came into view on the back of the flatbed.

"What's this?" George's face lit up.

"What does it look like?" Margaret hugged his neck. "Merry Christmas George!"

All George could do was stare at his sons as they removed the strapping and unloaded the sleigh.

"Remember this sleigh, Dad?" Anthony asked him. "It was at the farm where we picked up the Case tractor for restoration."

"Was the guy planning on selling it?"

"I told him you liked it and made him an offer."

George walked around the sleigh and inspected all of its features. On each side of the sleigh hung a battery operated lantern. George turned each lantern on and giggled. The sleigh was freshly painted red with a gold trace line along the top. On the front board was a brass rein rack and whip holder. Across the back of the sleigh, 'Sir William' was written in bold gold letters. Then he looked back at Anthony, grinning from ear to ear. "You bought this for me and restored it?"

Baron stepped closer to his father, "We all chipped in."

"Are you surprised, Pops?" Jim asked as he rolled up the strappings.

George stood with his mouth open, not knowing what to say.

Then Margaret quickly opened the barn doors and turned on the lights. "Merry Christmas!"

The three animals yawned and blinked their eyes from the lights. A red Christmas stocking hung on each stall door. On Sir William's bridle rack, there was something wrapped in Christmas paper. Sir William belonged to George. He was a retired Amish work mule, almost all black, and stood 17.2 hands.

"What's this?" He said to his big mule. Sir William looked away from George and focused his attention on the contents in his Christmas stocking.

Margaret and the three boys stood near George as he took the package from the bridle rack. The package made a jingle sound.

"Sleigh bells," he smiled and shook the package close to his ear.

"What's a sleigh without sleigh bells?" Jim commented.

"Thank you Guys." He gave each son a big hug, then hugged and kissed his wife.

The romantic moment was interrupted when all the animals began to nicker.

While George and Margaret treated the equines with carrots and apples from their stockings, the boys brought the sleigh into the barn.

"Dad and Mom, sit in the sleigh so we can get your picture," Anthony insisted.

George gently stepped into the freshly painted sleigh. He ran his hand across the new cushion seat, then beckoned to Margaret. The couple sat tall and proud while the boys snapped photos with their cell phones.

"All right, let's go in and eat," Baron insisted. "I have to get to the firehouse."

"I do miss the Santa scene on Christmas Eve," Margaret sighed as she carried the garlic bread to the table. "There was always so much to do and I loved every minute of it." She sighed, "but now on Christmas Eve we sit and watch Christmas movies."

"Not this year," George interrupted. "After dinner I'm taking a ride in my new sleigh." He put his hands forward and mimicked holding driving reins as he sang "Dashing through the snow, in a one horse open sleigh."

The family bowed their heads and said grace.

When dinner was finished, Anthony's cell phone rang. "It's Steve," he nodded to Jim before answering.

Jim took the last swallow of his soda and faced his brother waiting for the outcome.

"Steve said to start plowing the shelter. The driveway is long and steep and he wants to make sure it is plowed for the the firetruck."

"Tell Steve, the firehouse appreciates that," Baron said as he got up from the table.

"Good dinner, Mom," Jim gave his mother a hug, then gave his dad a pat on the back. "Be careful on the sleigh tonight."

Margaret rinsed the dishes as she watched her sons pull out the driveway and into the Christmas Eve night. George came up behind her and put his arms around her waist, "You did a good job raising those boys."

She chuckled, then cleared her throat. "Help me clean up so we can go for a sleigh ride."

George quickly turned back to the table and finished clearing it. When everything was cleaned, the couple bundled up and walked to the barn.

"Sir William, what do you think of your new sleigh?" George's eyes beamed as he gave the mule a treat from his Christmas stocking.

"If there are treats involved, I'm sure he is happy with his new sleigh." Margaret mumbled as she put rubber hoof boots on the mule to keep the snow from balling up in his feet. She began taking the harness out of the trunk, and handed the collar to George.

He held the collar up in front of Sir William. The mule obediently put his head through the cumbersome collar. "Good boy," George whispered to his mule, then adjusted the hams.

When the harness was in place, George put the sleigh bells

around Sir William's neck, then raised his chin with pride. "He's ready to be hooked up to his new sleigh."

Margaret climbed into sleigh and patted the seat for her husband to sit down. George giggled, then gingerly sat down beside her. With wide eyes and a bright smile, he ran his hand across the rein rack. He nudged Margaret and chuckled, "Let's turn on the lanterns."

Margaret took the reins and drove the mule into the pasture. George took a deep breath and sat back in the bench seat as the big mule walked confidently along the fence. He giggled like a school boy looking at his wife. "I always wanted to go for a sleigh ride."

Margaret put both reins in one hand and squeezed George's hand with the other hand. "Merry Christmas," she smiled sweetly.

Another romantic moment was short lived when the sound of a truck horn honked from the end of the driveway.

"Mom, Dad!" A frantic voice called out. "We need help!"

Margaret quickly turned the mule around and jogged back to the driveway where Barron was waiting.

"The firetruck couldn't make it up the hill to the shelter; the driveway is covered with ice," he shouted as they approached. "Can Sir William pull the sleigh through the fields and deliver the presents?"

George raised his chest and sat up straighter in the sleigh. "My mule will handle it."

Margaret looked at Baron, then back at George. "I….I…. I think it will be okay. Sir William is wearing his snow boots with metal grips on the bottom."

Baron and George stared at her, waiting for a further comment.

"Well what are we waiting for? Let's get the toys on the sleigh."

Baron's face lit up. "We are very organized, Mom. You'd be proud of us."

As Baron spoke, two firemen approached the driveway carrying large red plastic bags over their shoulders. One of the firemen, Joe, was Margaret's brother. He was also the fire chief.

Joe called to Baron. "There are still two more bags, a bike and two sleds. How will all this fit onto that sleigh?"

Baron and George turned to Margaret. "Mom can you make this work?"

"Somehow we will make it work. Help them get the rest of the things from the firetruck." Then she turned to her husband, "Get some baling twine and the scissors while I stay with the sleigh."

"We really appreciate this," Joe kissed his sister, then put an insulated bag in the sleigh. "Here's some hot chocolate and donuts for the ride."

Minutes later Sir William pulled his new red sleigh out the driveway filled with Christmas presents and a bicycle tied to the back. In tow were two red flyer sleds with bags of Christmas presents tied to them.

"Hold on a minute," Baron hollered and ran after them.

George brought his mule to a halt and waited.

"Santa hats," Baron panted as he handed a red wool hat with white fur to each of his parents. "Uncle Joe said to give these to you. He also said an officer will meet you at the traffic light so you can cross the highway."

As they began their journey along the snowy road, George

looked at Margaret with a wide grin and adjusted his hat. "Everyone is going to see my mule and think I am Santa Claus."

"Yeah, too bad Sir William doesn't have a red nose," Margaret laughed.

When they reached the traffic light, the officer acknowledged them with a wave. He turned on his red flashing lights and stoped the traffic.

People in their cars waved and shouted "Merry Christmas," as Sir William jogged across the highway with his jingling sleigh bells and Christmas treasures. George sat tall and proud in the seat holding the reins to the animal on spotlight. His smile was radiant; he nudged Margaret, "This is the best Christmas present ever."

She put one arm around her husband and waved to the people with the other hand.

After they crossed the highway, another officer greeted them. "Merry Christmas, Mrs. Margaret, " a young officer raised his chin and waved. "I am driving ahead of you to the shelter. The snow plows are leaving one side of the road snow covered for the sleigh."

"Merry Christmas, Dylan," Margaret waved then threw a kiss to the young officer, who used to play baseball with her son.

As Sir William merrily jogged down Main Street people came out of their houses to see what was going on.

"It's Santa and Mrs. Santa!" Voices cried from various directions. "I didn't know Rudolf had such big ears!" "Where are the rest of the reindeer?"

Margaret and George laughed with delight. She wrapped her arms around George's arm and snuggled closer to him.

As they got closer to the Episcopal Church, Sir William

brayed and picked up his pace. "It's the live Nativity Scene," Margaret declared. "He's calling to the donkey."

No sooner did she speak the words, and another loud bray filled the air. A donkey trotted out of the Bethlehem Stable with a little angel and a little shepherd boy running after him.

"It looks like we've got company," George chuckled and brought his mule to a stop.

By the time the donkey reached Sir William, St. Joseph caught up to him with a halter and lead line. Without saying a word, he removed his headpiece and gave it to the shepherd boy, then put the halter on the donkey and led the donkey back to the stable. Margaret and George watched as St. Joseph put his headpiece back on and the angel and the shepherd boy took their places.

They chuckled and continued down Main Street to the entrance of the shelter. The snow came down harder and the wind picked up. Dylan got out of his car and approached the sleigh while zipping up his coat. "It looks like it might be best for you to walk up along the other side of the snow fence where the drift has stopped."

George agreed and turned the mule up the driveway.

"I'll be right here waiting for you," Dylan shivered, then turned to his car.

Margaret and George rode silently as the big mule pulled the sleigh and Christmas cargo up the steep hill to the shelter. Sir William's hooves aggressively crunched through the frozen grass and snow. The lamps on the sleigh illuminated the mule's breath which became stronger as the hill became steeper. Not once did he hesitate or even slow his pace until he reached the top and the shelter house came into view.

"That is one beautiful farmhouse," Margaret whispered

without taking her eyes off the old fashion color lights that framed the long covered porch. A Christmas wreath decorated the front door and a view through the picture window displayed stockings hung from a mantle over a fireplace.

"What do we do now?" George whispered.

"I don't know. I don't see anyone. Do you?"

"No, I don't see anyone either." George looked around stretching his neck.

"Maybe everyone is asleep? There are no lights on upstairs, only one light downstairs." George thought for a moment then moved closer to the house. "Let's put the bags on the porch and get going."

George hopped out of the sleigh and put his hands on Sir William's shoulder. "He needs a blanket!"

"I've got one!" Margaret quickly wrapped a thick red blanket over the mule and tucked it in around his neck and under his tail.

He nuzzled Margaret's arm, then stood quietly while Margaret and George put the Christmas treasures on the porch. Before getting back in the sleigh, George checked his mule and secured his blanket.

As they descended down the hill to Main Street, George took Margaret's hand. "So you did get to deliver the presents after all."

"That was fun," she smiled and moved closer to him. "I didn't get to see their faces, but this was very special."

As they drove away with their backs to the shelter, they were unable to see a bedroom light turn on from the second story. A little boy whispered to his older brother, "I didn't know Rudolf wore a red coat!"

Dylan sighed with relief when he saw the sleigh. Margaret waved, then poured hot chocolate and took two donuts from the bag. She looked up and down the barren streets and sighed. "It looks like everyone has gone to bed."

Only Christmas lights illuminated the houses and the sidewalks. The wind died down and soft snowflakes continued to fall from the sky. Only the soothing sound of the mule's hoof beats in the snow could be heard through the silence.

When Sir William reached the Episcopal Church's Bethlehem Stable, he stopped and peered inside. The cast and crew were gone, leaving the Baby Jesus doll alone in the manger. The big mule took a tiny step closer to the manger. Then closed his eyes and bowed his head.

Merry Christmas.

Printed in the United States
by Baker & Taylor Publisher Services